The Jewish Joke

The Jewish Joke

A Short History—with Punchlines

Devorah Baum

PEGASUS BOOKS
NEW YORK LONDON

For Josh, Manny and Isaiah

THE JEWISH JOKE

Pegasus Books, Ltd.
148 West 37th Street, 13th Floor
New York, NY 10018

ISBN: 978-1-68177-742-9

10 9 8 7 6 5 4 3 2 1

Printed in the United States of America
Distributed by W. W. Norton & Company, Inc.

Contents

INTRODUCTION

LESS ESSAY, MORE EXAMPLES

AND FINALLY...

HOW DO YOU TELL THE DIFFERENCE BETWEEN A SHLEMIEL AND A SHLIMAZEL?

The Jewish joke is as old as Abraham. Like the Jews themselves, it has wandered over the world, learned various languages, worked with a range of different materials, and performed in front of some pretty hostile crowds. That it's been able, for the most part, to adapt and survive in ever-new pastures and among ever-new company is no mean feat. Jokes don't tend to travel all that well. And a lot of things that once seemed funny no longer are. Yet Jewish jokes, or a fair few of them, have had astonishing staying power. The popularity of a recent TV show, *Old Jews Telling Jokes*, plays up to this: the jokes and the jokers may be old, the show suggests, but they've still 'got it'. But *why* have they still got it? Is there no last laugh to be had? How old, really, can a joke get?

'There's an old joke,' Woody Allen's character Alvy says in the opening monologue of *Annie Hall* (1977):

> Uh, two elderly women are at a Catskills mountain resort, and one of 'em says, 'Boy, the food at this place is really terrible.' The other one says, 'Yeah, I know, and such ... small portions.' Well, that's essentially how I feel about life. Full of loneliness and misery and suffering and unhappiness, and it's all over much too quickly.

But what exactly *is* the old joke here? Is it the still-good punchline about 'such small portions'? Or is it the way of telling the joke so hesitantly that its punchline gets overwhelmed by the joker's neurosis? Are we laughing along with this comedian, or are we laughing at him? Are we laughing at the funny ha ha or at the funny peculiar? Or could it be something sadder we're finding funny? Might we be laughing, for instance, at how seriously the joke gets taken by a joker who has no sooner uttered it than he adds a commentary detailing an existential view of the world – one with a distinctly melancholic undertone?

'The-the other important joke for me,' Alvy falters on:

... is one that's, uh, usually attributed to Groucho Marx, but I think it appears originally in Freud's wit and its relation to the unconscious.[*] And it goes like this – I'm paraphrasing: Uh ... 'I would never wanna belong to any club that would have someone like me for a member.' That's the key joke of my adult life in terms of my relationships with women. Tsch, you know, lately the strangest things have been going through my mind, 'cause I turned forty, tsch, and I guess I'm going through a life crisis or something, I don't know. I, uh ... and I'm not worried about ageing. I'm not one o' those characters, you know. Although I'm balding slightly on top, that's about the worst you can say about me. I, uh, I think I'm gonna get better as I get older, you know? I think I'm gonna be the-the balding virile type, you know, as opposed to say the, uh, distinguished grey, for instance, you know? 'Less I'm neither o' those two. Unless I'm one o' those guys with saliva dribbling out of his mouth who wanders into a cafeteria with a shopping bag, screaming about socialism.

---

[*] Sigmund Freud's *Jokes and Their Relation to the Unconscious* (1905) is a sober study of the psychoanalysis of jokes and other uses of humour. Most of the jokes Freud offers by way of example are Jewish jokes.

That's some shtick: digressive, interpretative, remonstrative. And it's got a long memory too, treating an 'important joke' as if it were a piece of scripture to be traced back, first to its earlier comic source (Groucho), and then to an even earlier scholarly source (Freud – although I haven't spotted it there). But who on earth wants to hear shtick like that? Doesn't everyone know that jokes are best left at their punchlines? Nobody wants their jokes *explained*, do they? ... Unless explaining the joke is part of the joke – or part of the *Jewish* joke?

Alvy, above, makes no mention of Jewishness. Still, it's hard not to detect it in, for instance, the joke about belonging to clubs. For to get why this joker tells this joke in this particular way, by placing it within its Jewish heritage – Freud and (Groucho) Marx – you surely need an ironic sense of Jews as quintessentially members of a club to which they only really belong to the extent that they resist their membership. It's no accident, for example, that Alvy's life crisis has ensued because he can't make it work with a Jewish woman *or* with a shiksa (non-Jewish woman). Although if the shtick feels Jewish, then so too does the comedian himself, whose bespectacled face looms large and centre screen, eyes direct to camera, as if this were a joke on the cinema-going audience, who find themselves addressed by a less than obviously cinematic figure busily assuring them that he is a man in his prime, now and for ever the 'balding virile type'. Ha!

Of course, in 1977 Woody Allen was indeed a man in his prime, and he was taking the little respected art of comedy and turning it into something smart, serious and sublime. This he did with the comedian's gift for great timing. Just when the traditional frameworks and religious institutions of Jewish life were losing appeal for an upcoming generation determined to throw off the shackles of the old and substitute the new liberal order in all its lustre and complexity, Allen showed audiences that he knew and understood the critical value of time-keeping:

> I'm very proud of my gold pocket watch. My grandfather, on his deathbed, sold me this watch.*

> You look so beautiful I can hardly keep my eyes on the meter.**

> More than any other time in history, mankind faces a crossroads. One path leads to despair and utter

---

* *Stand Up Comic: 1964–1968.*
** *Manhattan* (1979).

hopelessness. The other, to total extinction. Let us pray we have the wisdom to choose correctly.[*]

He showed, in other words, that he had his finger on the pulse of not only the present moment but the historical one. Because it isn't *really* the gold watch or ticking meter that tells the value of time for the comedian. It's a feel for the audience's narrative expectations and the ability to confound these with a sudden reversal or change of direction: what's known in the gag trade as a switcheroo. So where we're expecting a gift we get a sale, where we're expecting romance we get realism, where we're expecting a positive we get a second negative. To wit, the comedian is the person who reveals this to us, reveals that things can change when you least expect them to.

And the times they *do* keep on changing. Thus, in the words of the young American comedian Lena Dunham:

Over time, my belief in many things has wavered: marriage, the afterlife, Woody Allen.[**]

[*] *New York Times*, 'My Speech to the Graduates' (1979).
[**] *Not That Kind of Girl: A Young Woman Tells You What She's 'Learned'* (2014).

Dunham's dismay at the clay feet of her comedy hero is palpable. Yet in saying so she also offers us a great line – a line reminiscent *of* Woody Allen, whose comic cadence it resembles while reminding us of Allen's main preoccupations: marriage, the afterlife, himself. So could this mean that – irony of ironies! – Allen *does* have an afterlife? Could all that Woodyish comedy – the sexual angst, the existential angst, the navel-gazing – have a young, hipster, *female* future?

When things reach crisis point, as they often do in Jewish history, it is Jewish custom to return to traditional sources for inspiration. According to the foundational text of Jewish mysticism, the Zohar, the biggest joke in the Hebrew Bible is the one when God tells Abraham to sacrifice his 'only son' Isaac. Isaac, whose name in Hebrew means 'laughter' on account of his mother Sarah's laughter upon learning at the age of ninety that she was about to become a parent for the first time – funny! – wasn't actually Abraham's 'only son'. He also had a son called Ishmael. Yet three times in the biblical story God insists that Isaac is the 'only one' to be sacrificed. Then, at the last moment, an angel stays Abraham's hand and recommends he sacrifices a ram in Isaac's place. So, a classic switcheroo. And boy oh boy, Abraham really fell for that one. The God of the Jews is clearly a prankster of the highest order. He's the God who laughs hard when, as the old joke goes, you tell Him your plans.

The darkly funny writer Franz Kafka detected in the same story a sort of blueprint for Jewish comedy. Once again, the joke is on Abraham, who now appears as less of a 'knight of faith' – as in the (also darkly funny) Protestant philosopher Søren Kierkegaard's sobriquet for him[*] – and more of a schlemiel. As Kafka tells it:

> It is as if, at the end of the year, when the best student was solemnly about to receive a prize, the worst student rose in the expectant stillness and came forward from his dirty desk in the last row because he had made a mistake of hearing, and the whole class burst out laughing. And perhaps he had made no mistake at all, his name really was called, it having been the teacher's intention to make the rewarding of the best student at the same time a punishment for the worst one.[**]

---

[*] Though in claiming that one arrives at Abrahamic faith 'by virtue of the absurd', Kierkegaard's *Fear and Trembling* (1843) clearly sees some humour in the escapade too.

[**] This can be found in Kafka's *Parables and Paradoxes in German and English* (Schocken Books, 1961).

Kafka's Abe has been singled out not for praise but for derision. He's the total shlemiel who, as he proudly walks to the front of the class to accept his 'prize', doesn't yet realise that the other kids are already laughing at the 'kick me' sign stuck to his back.

So is *that* – a sort of 'Bathos 101' – what explains the miraculous longevity of the Jewish joke? Does the full pantheon of Jewish comedy with all its parading fools – its shmucks, shlemiels, shlimazels, shnorrers, shmendricks, (sh)mothers (Yiddish has as many terms for fool as there are Inuit words for snow) – ramp up these various differences simply in order to disguise the overarching fact that any and every Jew answering to the name is not only 'in' on the joke, but the butt of it?

Or to put it slightly differently:

Q: How *do* you tell the difference between a shlemiel and a shlimazel?

A: The shlemiel is the one who slips up and spills his soup *over* the shlimazel.*

---

* From the Yiddish *shlim* (bad, wrong) and *mazl* (luck). While in America the use of the Yiddish word *shlimazel* nearly always alludes to a born loser, in Britain you'll just as often find it referring to a messy situation. In June 2004 *shlimazel* was voted one of the ten hardest-to-translate non-English words by a British translation company.

And in a joke, a little slip can make all the difference. Not that you can put limits on slipperiness. For as different as we may well be from each other, we're all, surely, alike in this: our identities are not so much fixed, as a matter of where it is we happen to be standing in relation to everyone else at any given time. Hence if, as Kafka has it, Jews are history's greatest shlemiels, then that doesn't make them *so* different. What it makes them is one half of an eternally returning comedy double act in which, as we'll see, all other Jews, Gentiles, the Chinese and *even* God can't help getting a little soupy.

The Chinese?

Yes. Jews distinguish Chinese people from all other Gentiles on account of a) China being a very long way away from where most Jews find themselves standing, and b) the privileged position of Chinese cuisine within the Jewish *Weltanschauung* (Jews may abandon Jewish dietary laws when inside Chinese restaurants alone):

> A Jewish man and a Chinese man were conversing. The Jewish man commented upon what a wise people the Chinese are.

'Yes,' replied the Chinese man, 'our culture is over four thousand years old. But you Jews are a very wise people, too.'

The Jewish man replied, 'Yes, our culture is over five thousand years old.'

The Chinese man was incredulous. 'That's impossible,' he replied. 'Where did your people eat for a thousand years?'

More recently, however, the Chinese have also been introduced to Jewish cuisine:

Upon leaving a kosher restaurant, one Chinese diner says to another: 'The problem with Jewish food is that two days later you're hungry again."

---

* The jokes I've included in this book belong to two categories: those that illustrate the arguments of the essay and those, like this one, that have no obvious place in the essay but were too good to leave out.

HOW DO YOU TELL THE DIFFERENCE BETWEEN ONE JEW AND ANOTHER JEW?

You'll have heard it said that wherever you can find two Jews, you'll find at least three opinions. It's because Jews don't only disagree with Gentiles, or with each other, they don't even agree with themselves:

A Jew is shipwrecked on a desert island. Years later, a passing ship notices his campfire and stops to rescue him. When the captain comes ashore, the castaway thanks him profusely and offers to give him a tour of the little island. He shows off the weapons he made for hunting, the fire pit where he cooks his food, the synagogue he built for praying in, the hammock

where he sleeps. On their way back to the ship,
however, the captain notices a second synagogue. 'I
don't understand,' the captain asks; 'why build two
synagogues?' 'This,' says the Jew, motioning to one, 'is
the synagogue I pray in, and this,' he motions at the
other, 'is the synagogue I wouldn't be seen dead in.'

What is quintessentially Jewish? It's being at odds
with oneself. It's taking pride in one's difference
and feeling ashamed of it at the same time. Hence,
perhaps, why self-deprecation plays such a key role in
Jewish joking – so much so, in fact, that Freud could
ponder 'whether there are many other instances
of a people making fun to such a degree of its own
character'.

And yet the funniest thing about Jewish self-
deprecation is the pride that Jews are wont to take
in it:

It is the Yom Kippur service and the cantor suddenly
stops mid-prayer and declares, 'Forgive me, God!
I can't say this! I'm just a nothing!' Later the rabbi,
mid-sermon, stops and cries, 'Forgive *me*, God! *I*
am not worthy! *I'm* only a nothing!' Seeing this, the
synagogue's caretaker charges from the back of the
synagogue. 'If you two great men are unworthy to

beseech God, then what right have I, as someone so ordinary? I'm a complete nothing! Oy vey, am I a nothing!' At which point the rabbi taps the cantor on the shoulder: '*Look* who thinks he's nothing.'

No two nothings are ever quite the same. Thus the joker's modest pose is assumed, the better to distance the joker from the real butt of her joke – always those *other* Jews whom she doesn't resemble in the least:

A woman is riding a bus in the Midwest, when a man gets on the bus and sits down next to her. He's wearing a black hat, long black coat, black trousers and shoes, and he has a long curly dark beard.

The woman looks at him with disgust. 'Jews like you,' she hisses at him.

He looks up at her, puzzled, and says, 'I beg your pardon, madam?'

She says, 'Look at you. All in black, a beard, never take off your hat! It's Jews like you that give the rest of us a bad name.'

'I beg your pardon, madam, but I am not Jewish. I'm Amish.'

The woman suddenly smiles, 'Oh, how *darling*! You've kept your customs.'

It's a Jewish joke, in effect, *about* the Jewish joke – about the types of jokes that assimilated Western Jews have historically told to denigrate and thus distance themselves from their poorer relatives, the so-called *Ostjuden* (Jews from the East). Indeed, given how often Jewish jokes seem to turn on such divisions and doublings within Jewish identity, one wonders if Jewishness itself mightn't be structured like a joke.

Of what such a suggestion might mean, there's more in the rest of the book. But for now let's simply note that, *like* jokes, Jews love nothing more than telling the difference between things – and especially each other:

Q: How do you tell the difference between one Jew and another Jew?

A: Wait, wait. They'll tell *you*.

HOW DO YOU TELL THE DIFFERENCE BETWEEN A JEW AND A GENTILE?

There are occasions, though, when Jews *do* form a collective identity:

> Back in the day, two Jews, Moishe and Itzik, are walking in the Ukrainian forest. In the distance, they see two local guys walking towards them. Moishe turns to Itzik, panics, and says, 'Itzik, what should we do? There's two of them, and we're all alone!'

There are a great many candidates for the world's most Jewish joke, but this one, for me, tops the list. Because there they are, those proverbial 'two Jews' – all alone in a big bad world, feeling weak and outnumbered (regardless of their strength or numbers), as two non-Jews (brute simpletons,

obviously) approach them ... Ahhhh! Danger! Help!
What are two all-alone Jews expected to do in such a
dastardly situation? Tell jokes?

Well, yes, as it happens. Here, for example, are
those same two Jews encountering difficulties again:

Two Jews, driving a wagon along a narrow road,
come to a place where boulders are blocking their
path. They sit, considering what to do, discussing
each of their options in great detail. Suddenly two
Gentiles come along in another wagon, jump out of
their seat, roll up their sleeves and push the boulders
off the road.

'There, that's goyish thinking for you,' says one of the
Jews, 'always with the might.'

Here, on the other hand, is Jewish thinking for you:

A Jewish woman in a hospital tells the doctor she
wants to be transferred to a different hospital.

The doctor says, 'What's wrong? Is it the food?'

'No, the food is fine. I can't kvetch [complain].'

'Is it the room?'

'No, the room is fine. I can't kvetch.'

'Is it the staff?'

'No, everyone on the staff is fine. I can't kvetch.'

'Then why do you want to be transferred?'

'I can't kvetch!'

Kvetching is that special type of pleasure to be elicited from complaining even when things go right – because if there's one thing Jews can be sure of, it's that there's *always* a negative.

And, as we'll discover, there are reasons for that. For it's not only that Jews love to kvetch, they also take a pretty dim view of the world:

Q: How many Jewish mothers does it take to change a lightbulb?

A: That's OK, don't trouble yourself, we'll sit in the dark.

Given the ordeal that characterises so much of Jewish history, it's hardly surprising if Jews *do* tend to see things darkly (not to mention the expense to be spared when the lights are turned off). But what jokes like these also show is that, while an intolerable heaviness has been the burden of Jewish history, it's a heaviness accompanied by an irreverent levity whose aim it is to make that intolerable heaviness a little more, well, tolerable:

> Two Jews sat in a coffeehouse, discussing the fate of their people.
>
> 'How miserable is our history,' said one. 'Pogroms, plagues, discrimination, Hitler, neo-Nazis ... Sometimes I think we'd be better off if we'd never been born.'
>
> 'Sure,' said his friend. 'But who has that much luck, maybe one in ten thousand?'

So it's not for nothing that the waiter must ask of the Jewish diners, 'Is *anything* all right?' Though the waiter's question is best considered alongside the

---

* Hard to resist, though precisely the kind of borderline anti-Semitic joke that only Jews can reasonably expect to get away with.

jokes Jews sometimes like to tell about their comedy counterparts – those peculiarly unflappable creatures known as 'Gentiles' …

Two Gentiles run into one another in the street.

'Hi, John. How are you?'

'Oh, hello, Freddie. I'm fine, thanks.'

Jews find that one side-splittingly funny. And this one …

A Gentile calls his mother.

'Hello, Mum.'

'Hi, darling.'

'I can't come over for dinner tonight after all.'

'OK. See you soon.'

Hilarious!

As for the mothers of *Jews*, still sitting there, lightbulb-less, in the dark ('Honestly, we're fine like this, you go ahead and enjoy yourself ...'), well, at least they have each other to kvetch with:

'Oy,' says one.

'Oy vey,' sighs a second.

'Nu,' shrugs the third.

At this, the fourth gets up from her chair, glowering. 'I thought we'd agreed *not* to talk about our children!'

HOW DO YOU TELL THE DIFFERENCE BETWEEN A JEWISH PERSON AND A COMEDIAN?

Remember that episode of *Seinfeld* when Jerry's dentist converts to Judaism?* Jerry is seated in his dentist's chair, and his dentist tells him a (not very good) Jewish joke about matzo balls:

> Jerry: 'Do you think you should be making jokes like that?'
>
> Dentist: 'Why not, I'm Jewish, remember? Jerry, it's our sense of humour that sustained us as a people for three thousand years.'

* 'The Yada Yada' (TV episode, 1997).

Jerry: 'Five thousand.'

Dentist: 'Five thousand – even better.'

His dentist, Jerry figures, shouldn't get to tell Jewish jokes – you need millennia of persecution to have a sense of humour like that (though, you have to admit, 'Five thousand – even better' *is* a pretty good Jewish joke). But does Jerry really have the right to kvetch? For while having badly-told Jewish jokes visited upon you while supine in your dentist's chair is no picnic, Jerry hasn't *personally* suffered so much of that history of persecution. Yet there's something about his dentist's conversion to Judaism that troubles him. What, he suspects, his dentist may *really* be after is the holy grail of comedy: 'total joke-telling immunity'. Getting to tell any joke he likes. Which is such chutzpah, it's enough to lead Jerry to a confession box to grass on the dentist to his former priest:

Jerry: 'I have a suspicion that he converted to Judaism only for the jokes.'

Father: 'And this offends you as a Jewish person?'

Jerry: 'No, it offends me as a comedian!'

And if you remain unsure *how* exactly to tell the difference between a Jewish person and a comedian, then you're probably getting what I take to be the point of the whole episode: it isn't so easy to tell.

In fact, when his dentist first announces his conversion, Jerry's response – 'Welcome aboard!' – is less offended, or delighted, than bemused. If, indeed, *anything* tells the difference between Judaism and the major monotheisms to which it's most often compared, this could well be it: while Christians and Muslims tend to regard converts to their faith as serious people of good sense, Jews harbour a sneaking suspicion that the would-be Jewish convert must be joking.

Although if Jews often have a hard time accepting why anyone would want to convert *to* Judaism, they're usually even less accepting of those who attempt to convert *out* of it:

Two Jews are strolling down the street one day in the Pale of Settlement, when they happen to walk past a church. Above the door of the church they see a big sign that says 'Convert and get ten rubles'. Moishe stops, stares at the sign and turns to his friend:

'Avreleh, I'm thinking of doing it.' With that, he strides purposefully into the church. Twenty minutes later he comes out with his head bowed.

'So', asks Avrelch, 'did you get your ten rubles?'

Moishe looks at him contemptuously: 'Is that *all* you people think about?'

Which is surely one of the best jokes, let alone Jewish jokes, of all time, because it demonstrates so neatly how power really works.

And such jokes also help to explain why Jews, historically, have often viewed conversion as a sociopolitical rather than authentically religious phenomenon:

Four converts trade stories about why they converted. The first claims he was a victim of a false accusation and converted to escape the harsh sentence he would otherwise have had to serve. The second confesses that her parents drove her wild with complaints about her lax observance, so she converted to spite them. The third gives a rambling account of falling in love with a Christian boy: she converted in order to marry him. The fourth pipes up: 'Unlike the rest of you, I converted out of a firm conviction that Christianity is a religion of a higher order.'

'Oh, PLEASE!' the others interrupt him. 'Save that for your goyishe friends!'

Which suspicion of conversion has lingered even when Jews have turned to other religions during more liberal times:

My best friend is a Jewish Buddhist. Believes you should renounce all material possessions but still keep the receipts. *David Baddiel*

So you think you can cease to be Jewish, huh? Well then, the joke's on you:

Mr Dropkin was on a business trip in a small town and was giving his major presentation on the stage when he bent over and gave the loudest fart anyone had ever heard. He never showed up in that small town again. But many, many, many years later he was invited back. Undecided whether or not he could yet show his face, he tried to coax himself: 'I'm so old now,' he thought. 'Surely no one will remember me from all those years ago. I don't even look as I did then.' So he decided to return. All the same, when checking into the hotel he took the precaution of changing his name.

'Have you ever visited our pretty town before?' the hotel receptionist asked him, genially.

'Only once,' said Mr Dropkin. 'But it was a long time ago and between you and me I haven't returned until now because I've always been so embarrassed about a very painful experience that happened to me when I was here, and have feared that people might still remember it.'

'Oh, what a shame!' said the receptionist, before reassuring him, 'you know, people have such short memories and they're really only focused on their own lives – things are never quite so bad as you think. So I'm sure you're being paranoid. I mean, how long ago *was* this incident?'

Dropkin said he didn't exactly remember.

'Well, was it before or after the Dropkin fart?'

HOW DO YOU TELL THE DIFFERENCE BETWEEN A JEW AND A PARROT?

We can think of the Dropkin fart as a metaphor for Jewish history: however much Jews try to repress their origins, they've learned the hard way that what they thought was past always returns to embarrass them by slipping out one way or the other:

A Jew converts and becomes a priest. He gives his first Mass in front of a number of high-ranking priests who came for the occasion. At the end of the new priest's sermon a cardinal goes to congratulate him. 'Father Goldberg,' he says, 'that was very well done, you were just perfect. Just one little thing. Next time, try not to start your sermon with 'My fellow goyim ...'

It can happen anywhere:

> James and Gracie Carter put on their finest clothes and head out to one of London's swankiest restaurants for their anniversary dinner. The waiter hands them the menu. James looks it over as if a habitué.
>
> 'And what would sir like for his main?' the waiter asks.
>
> 'Whatever you recommend,' says James dismissively, 'just so long as it's treyf [non-kosher].'
>
> 'Oy vey!' exclaims a nearby diner ... 'Whatever *that* means.'

It's a problem that Jews have even had to contend with in the *new* world – the reason, for example, why the Cohens of Boston decided to name their newborn son Luke Lincoln Cohen because *Abraham* Lincoln sounded too Jewish.

What such jokes – and there are many of them – seem to suggest is that there's something unshakeable about Jewishness. 'When you wake up,' the American comedian Judy Gold was once asked, 'do you feel more Jewish or more lesbian?'

I always feel Jewish. I get up and my back hurts, I've got to go to the bathroom, I've got to have a coffee. I'm a Jew. I don't wake up and go, 'Oh, my God, that girl's hot.' It's 'I gotta put some beans in the coffee thing. Should I make oatmeal? I need to go to the gym – no, I don't feel like going.' I wake up like an elderly Jew in assisted living.[*]

A new day it may be, but still there's the same old tsores (troubles, sufferings, oy oy oys) – and it's *that* (plus the vague distrust of the coffee 'thing') that feels Jewish.

Which isn't, of course, to deny that other people have their tsores too:

A formerly religious young man is attending Oxford University. When his father, with a long beard, skull-cap and side curls, comes to visit him, he is filled with shame and tells his father in no uncertain terms that he feels all his success at fitting in at one of Britain's elite institutions will be undone by this spectacle of difference. Wanting to aid his son, his father heads for a barber and has his side curls removed, his beard shaved off, and he even takes off his skullcap. At that point his father bursts into tears. Profoundly moved,

* Interview for *Out Magazine* (2016).

his son says, 'But, Father, I never meant for you to lose your identity entirely. I just wanted you to minimise your difference, not obliterate it. I'm so sorry for the pain I've caused you.'

'No, no, it's not that,' says his father, 'I'm crying because we lost India.'

Oy oy oy indeed.

But even when a Jew, such as the man weeping openly for the loss not of his side curls, but of India, does genuinely appear to have recalibrated his identity, the lesson of the Dropkin fart may still apply. Thus, if we say, for the sake of argument, that a Jew wakes up, goes to the bathroom, has coffee and oatmeal, and is looking and acting much like anyone else by the time they're on the street, even then there's usually some other Jew threatening to expose them. As Freud tells it:

A Galician Jew was travelling in a train. He had made himself very comfortable, had unbuttoned his coat and put his feet up on the seat. Just then a gentleman in modern dress entered the compartment. The Jew promptly pulled himself together and took up a proper pose. The stranger fingered through the pages in a notebook, made some calculations, reflected for a moment and then suddenly asked the Jew, 'Excuse me, when is Yom Kippur [the Day of Atonement]?'

'Oho!' said the Jew, relaxing entirely, and put his feet up before answering.

But, who is the butt of the joke here? Is it the old-world Jew as seen through the eyes of his assimilated cousin, or isn't the Galician Jew just another shlemiel making a shlimazel out of the straight guy?

A woman on a train leans over to another passenger. 'Excuse me,' she says, 'but are you Jewish?'

'No,' replies the man.

A few minutes later she asks again. 'Excuse me,' she says, 'are you sure you're not Jewish?'

'I'm sure,' says the man.

But the woman's unconvinced, and a few minutes later she inquires a third time. 'Are you absolutely sure you're not Jewish?'

'All right, all right,' the man says. 'You win. I'm Jewish.'

'That's funny,' says the woman.' You don't look Jewish.'

For who but a Jew would dream of showing so little sign of it?

Then again, Jews are liable to find equally suspect the Jew who appears *not* to be hiding:

> Two rivals meet in the Warsaw train station. 'Where are you going?' says the first.
>
> 'To Minsk,' says the second.
>
> 'To Minsk, eh? What a nerve! I know you're telling me you're going to Minsk because you want me to think that you're really going to Pinsk. But it so happens that I know you really *are* going to Minsk. So … why are you lying to me?'

So you're telling the truth? Well, isn't *that* a good disguise!

Jokes about Jews on a train are jokes about Jews as passengers – as people who are always attempting to pass … go along with … assimilate … parody … *parrot* …

Meyer, a lonely widower, was walking home one night when he passed a pet store and heard a squawking voice shouting out in Yiddish, 'Quawwwwk … vus machst du … yeah, du … outside, standing like a shlemiel … eh?'

Meyer rubbed his eyes and ears. He couldn't believe it. The proprietor sprang out of the door and grabbed Meyer by the sleeve. 'Come in here, fella, and check out this parrot.'

Meyer stood in front of an African Grey that cocked his little head and said, 'Vus? Ir kent reddin Yiddish?'

Meyer turned excitedly to the store owner. 'He speaks Yiddish?'

In a matter of moments, Meyer had placed five hundred dollars down on the counter and carried the parrot in his cage away with him. All night he talked with the parrot in Yiddish. He told the parrot about his father's adventures coming to America, about how beautiful his mother was when she was a young bride, about his family, about his years of working in the garment centre, about Florida. The parrot listened and commented. They shared some walnuts.

The parrot told him of living in the pet store, how he hated the weekends. Finally, they both went to sleep.

Next morning, Meyer began to put on his tefillin [phylacteries], all the while saying his prayers. The parrot demanded to know what he was doing, and when Meyer explained, the parrot wanted to do it too. Meyer went out and made a miniature set of tefillin for the parrot. The parrot wanted to learn to daven [pray], so Meyer taught him how to read Hebrew, and taught him every prayer in the Siddur with the appropriate nusach [version] for the daily services. Meyer spent weeks and months sitting and teaching the parrot the Torah, Mishnah and Gemara. In time, Meyer came to love and count on the parrot as a friend and a Jew.

On the morning of Rosh Hashanah, Meyer rose, got dressed and was about to leave when the parrot demanded to go with him. Meyer explained that shul [synagogue] was not a place for a bird, but the parrot made a terrific argument and was carried to shul on Meyer's shoulder. Needless to say, they made quite a sight when they arrived at the shul, and Meyer was questioned by everyone, including the rabbi and cantor, who refused to allow a bird into the building on the High Holy Days. However, Meyer convinced them to let him in this one time, swearing that the parrot could daven.

Wagers were made with Meyer. Thousands of dollars were bet that the parrot could NOT daven, could not speak Yiddish or Hebrew, and so on. All eyes were on the African Grey during services. The parrot perched on Meyer's shoulder as each prayer and song passed – Meyer heard not a peep from the bird. He began to become annoyed, slapping at his shoulder and mumbling under his breath, 'Daven!'

Nothing.

'Daven ... Feigelleh, please! You can daven, so daven ... come on, everybody's looking at you!'

Nothing.

After Rosh Hashanah services were concluded, Meyer found that he owed his shul buddies and the rabbi several thousand dollars. He marched home quite upset, saying nothing. Finally, several blocks from the shul, the bird, happy as a lark, began to sing an old Yiddish song. Meyer stopped and looked at him.

'You miserable bird, you cost me over four thousand dollars. Why? After I made your tefillin, taught you the morning prayers and taught you to read Hebrew and the Torah. And after you begged me to bring you to shul on Rosh Hashanah, why? Why did you do this to me?'

'Don't be a shlemiel,' the parrot replied. 'You know what odds we'll get at Yom Kippur?'

What kind of Jewishness is the parrot parroting? Not, it seems, the official text – the liturgy, the language and the law – but the subtext – the ghetto, street-smart survival instinct and adaptability. *Convert and get ten rubles!* Or, as Groucho Marx had it:

These are my principles! If you don't like them, I have others.

Hard not to laugh at such a luminous line. Still, there is, undeniably, a problem here: the problem as to why so many Jewish jokes and jokers depict Jews as charlatans or liars – so sneaky that even the honest ones are condemned as duplicitous. For if even Jews don't trust each other, what are non-Jews meant to make of them? Aren't Jewish jokes then guilty of *stoking* anti-Semitism?

In some cases, perhaps they are. But we can equally hear these same jokes, alongside Groucho's quips, as engaged in something more subtle: by joking about the slipperiness of the Jew, what such jokes also describe is the inherent slipperiness of the outsider's position. For in order to fit in with the dominant social group, the parrot will try to imitate the language of its hosts so as to get noticed, establish lines of communication and have its needs met. So if even for the *parrot* parroting is essentially a survival strategy, then the same, surely, may be assumed of the parroting Jew.

Do jokes about the slipperiness of Jewish identities appear less damning, then, if considered in such terms? The line to be drawn here is nothing if not blurry. Because it's true: when jokes about Jews attempting to pass are told by non-Jews, they *do* sound suspiciously similar to anti-Semitic ones. And actually, come to think of it ...

HOW DO YOU TELL THE DIFFERENCE BETWEEN A JEW AND AN ANTI-SEMITE?

The anti-Semite thinks the Jews are a despicable race, but Cohen? He's not too bad actually. Kushner? A stand-up guy. The Jew, on the other hand, believes his people are a light unto the nations, but Cohen? What a shmuck! Kushner? Don't get me started!

So when it comes to telling the difference, even here we're in the realm of the slippery. And thus the same may be said of the difference between a Jewish joke and an anti-Semitic one. For while some Jewish jokes seem to manifest an internalised anti-Semitism, others poke fun at the anti-Semitism they parrot:

Rabbi Altmann and his secretary were sitting in a coffeehouse in Berlin in 1935. 'Herr Altmann,' said his secretary, 'I notice you're reading *Der Stürmer*! I can't understand why. A Nazi libel sheet! Are you some kind of masochist, or, God forbid, a self-hating Jew?'

'On the contrary, Frau Epstein. When I used to read the Jewish papers, all I learned about were pogroms, riots in Palestine, and people leaving the faith in America. But now that I read *Der Stürmer*, I see so much more: that the Jews control all the banks, dominate in the arts and are on the verge of taking over the entire world. You know – it makes me feel a whole lot better.'

Jews have got rather used to hearing that they're responsible for all the world's problems. And not only the man-made ones, the natural ones too:

'Did you hear that Jews sunk the *Titanic*?'

'The Jews? I thought it was an iceberg.'

'Iceberg, Goldberg, Rosenberg, they're all the same.'

But even during the worst of times they've found ways to joke:

> Cohen lives in Berlin in 1933. He's walking along the street when Hitler drives up in a Volkswagen and leaps out with a Luger pistol in his hand. 'Get down in the gutter and eat the filth like the dog you are, Jew!' he snarls.

> Cohen has no choice. He obeys and eats the filth. Hitler starts laughing at the sight so hard that he drops the gun. Cohen snatches it up. 'Your turn, mein Führer,' he says, and points to the gutter.

> Later that night, Cohen comes home. His wife asks how his day went.

> 'Oh, so-so … But you'll never guess who I had lunch with today …'

Although, as we find in the following dialogue from Woody Allen's film *Deconstructing Harry* (1997), one can't always tell if the joker *is* even joking:

> Burt: 'Do you care even about the Holocaust, or do you think it never happened?'

Harry: 'Not only do I know that we lost six million, but the scary thing is that records are made to be broken.'

HOW DO YOU TELL THE DIFFERENCE BETWEEN JOKING AND NOT JOKING?

When Jerry's dentist proclaims, with the zeal of the newly converted, that 'it's our sense of humour that sustained us', he may make *us* laugh, but he isn't joking. Though to truly appreciate his formula for funniness – the more suffering you've had, the funnier you get to be – you'd need to look not to the minor irritations that rankle the cast of *Seinfeld*, but to Jewish life in the kind of pogrom-prone place where it's not always that easy to tell the difference between what *is* and isn't a joke:

> 'Good news! Good news! The child that got killed in the forest yesterday? He's Jewish!'

The 'joke'? That one murdered Jewish child in the forest may be counted 'good news' when contrasted with the pogrom liable to follow the discovery of a murdered Christian child. Sometimes we laugh, in other words, when we recognise a (terrible) truth. Or when we realise that what we're hearing *should* be a joke, but isn't.

We tend to think of wit as a form of levity, but as even the joke's own vocabulary attests, there are darker, more aggressive sides to humour. Consider the word *punchline*, for instance, with its suggestion that someone, by the end of the joke, is guaranteed to get knocked out. How should we understand such a 'technical' term? Do jokes necessarily require victims?

In the annals of Jewish joking we can see why punchlines might make sense:

> Mendel the butcher is walking to his store one morning when a stranger runs up, punches him in the face and says, 'That's for you, Yossel.'
>
> Mendel is surprised, but quickly starts to laugh.
>
> The stranger says, 'Why are you laughing? Do you want me to punch you again?'

Mendel says, 'No, it's just that the joke's on you – I'm not Yossel!'

When life's bound to beat you one way or another, you get your laughs however you can.

Though 'having a laugh' clearly isn't the only thing going on here. In Israeli author David Grossman's novel, *A Horse Walks into a Bar* (2017), set in a comedy club in which a stand-up comedian intersperses stock-in-trade gags within a much more disquieting monologue, it's the propensity to self-harm that first sets his audience on edge: 'He gives his forehead a loud, unfathomably powerful smack … It was an awful blow, that slap. An outburst of unexpected violence, a leakage of murky information'. And as the comedy swerves towards the painfully testimonial, our narrator, watching him, begins to understand what that murky information is: 'he is uniting with his abuser. Beating himself with another man's hands.' Thus what we see in the novel, rather like its pictured audience of repelled but fascinated spectators, is a sort of disrobing of the entire comedic project: instead of a comedian telling 'cracks' and the audience 'cracking up', his 'cracks' reveal deeper cracks as roles are reversed and it's the man on stage who cracks up.

Joking has always been a good cover for not joking. When speaking 'only in jest', one may speak of unspeakable things. The Holocaust survivor and novelist Aharon Appelfeld has written of how immediately after the war the victims of the camps were unable to talk about their experiences with each other directly *other* than through grotesque comic performances. Rather than thinking of comedy as tragedy plus time,* he found that comedy was the language that instinctively came first – possibly because it was the only genre that acknowledged the sheer impossibility of representing what the victims had lived through...

A Holocaust survivor gets up to heaven, meets God.

He tells God a Holocaust joke: God doesn't laugh.

The survivor shrugs: I guess you had to be there.

The child of a Holocaust survivor, David Schneider has long since been interested in the curious compulsion of so many jokers to find the laughs in

---

* A popular definition of comedy that has been attributed to various people but was most probably coined in the 1950s by Steve Allen, an American TV personality.

those things that clearly aren't in any straightforward sense 'funny':

> As a comedian, I've always been fascinated by whether you can do comedy about such a difficult and taboo subject.
>
> I used to compere Jewish comedy gigs and I remember once getting a note passed to me backstage saying: 'We are a coach party of Auschwitz survivors come to see you. Please can you say hello to us during the gig?'
>
> And I just thought, what am I meant to do? Go on and shout: 'Hi, is there anybody from Auschwitz in the place tonight?'

Thus, while it's understandable when people prefer not to laugh at such horrors, or feel shocked when others do, it would be a mistake to assume too much about anyone's laughter. Laughter, after all, frequently assails its subjects unbidden, implying that there may be things folded into it that aren't always known or recognised by the one who laughs. What's more, by paying attention to the alternative ways there always are of viewing even the darkest things, seeing the funny side is a skill worth having – not only for its ability to leaven our bleakest moments, but because it can help to identify blind spots, multiply perspectives and even create new possibilities. As such, there may be little to wonder at in the thought that Jews, wishing to expand the often narrowest of horizons, have so often depended on the funny. After all, there's nothing so bad that it can't get worse:

> Two Jews are in front of a firing squad awaiting their execution. As they stand there, the leader of the firing squad asks them, 'Do either of you have any last requests?'
>
> The first Jew says, 'There's been a terrible mistake!'
>
> The second Jew turns to him and whispers, 'Morris, don't make trouble.'

Nor anything so innocuous that it won't prove malign:

> An Englishman, a Scotsman and a Jew are sitting on a park bench.

The Englishman says, 'I am so tired and thirsty, I must have beer.'

The Scotsman says, 'I am so tired and thirsty, I must have whisky.'

The Jew says, 'I am so tired and thirsty, I must have diabetes.'

Nor any response so enthusiastic that it doesn't reveal a criticism:

A Jewish mother gives her son two neckties for his birthday. The boy hurries into his bedroom, rips off the tie he's wearing, puts on one of the ties his mother has brought him, and hurries back.

'Look, Mama! Isn't it gorgeous?'

His mother responds, 'What's the matter? You don't like the other one?'

Which is a bit of a mood-killer admittedly, and yet it's in precisely this nit-picking response that we can identify the lesson of Jewish history, along with that of the joke: there's always a flipside.

HOW DO YOU TELL THE DIFFERENCE BETWEEN A BLESSING AND A CURSE?

That the Jews who can spot the cheerier side of bad news can also spot the gloomier side of good news explains the deliciously contrarian spite to be found in typical Yiddish curses:

> 'May you become so rich that you're the richest person in your whole family!'

> 'May you become so rich that your wife's second husband never has to work a day in his life!'

Indeed, the standard response of today's average teenager upon hearing anything positive – 'good luck with *that* – has long since been the standard Jewish blessing: 'Mazel tov!' (literally 'good luck' rather than, as is more commonly translated, 'congratulations'). And certainly nothing gets a Jew down like 'positive thinking':

A group of Jews are discussing the state of the world:

'The economy is crashing and you know who they'll blame for it, don't you?'

'Have you *seen* the things they've been saying about us on social media?'

'Everyone's an anti-Semite. Trust nobody.'

'They always claim it's our fault.'

'Or Israel's fault.'

'What's *wrong* with you people? Why can't you be a bit more positive? Me, I'm an optimist!'

'You look pretty anxious for an optimist.'

'You think it's *easy* being an optimist?'

For most of their long history in the Diaspora, Jews have not had the resources to become warriors for their cause. As such, they've become worriers for their cause:

The citizens of Chelm [fantasy shtetl of Jewish joking lore] used to spend a good deal of time worrying – so much time, in fact, that they soon began to worry about how much they worried.

The Grand Council of Wise Men convened a meeting to discuss all this worrying, and to find a solution for it. For seven days and seven nights the wise men of Chelm discussed the problem, until finally the chairman announced a solution: Yossel, the chimney sweep, would be the official Chelm Worrier. In return for one ruble a week, he would do the worrying for everybody in Chelm. The Grand Council members all agreed that this was the ideal solution, but just before the vote was taken, one of the sages rose to speak against the proposal.

'Wait a minute,' he announced. 'If Yossel were to be paid one ruble a week, then what would he have to worry about?'

Still, Jews try not to worry until the optimal moment:

> The astronomer was concluding a lecture: 'Some believe the sun will die out within about four or five billion years.'
>
> '*How* many years did you say?' asked Mrs Shindler.
>
> 'Four or five billion.'
>
> 'Phew!' she replied, 'I thought you said *million*!'

And they can usually spot when the tides are turning and the signs are looking good:

> Two Jewish POWs are about to be shot. Suddenly the order comes to hang them instead. One smiles to the other: 'You see? They're running out of bullets.'

Telling the blessing from the curse, in other words, is really a matter of where you lay the emphasis – just as, no matter how good the joke you're about to utter may be, it'll fall flat on its face if you don't intone it right.

But while such jokes are obviously funny, they do more than merely amuse. For the laughter that hinges on surprise – for example, at the sudden reversal of meaning when a hanging becomes evidence of a bullet shortage – reminds whoever hears it that it's possible to *be* surprised. And that, interestingly, is something the joke shares with the messianic structure of the story that Jews tell of their own history. Indeed, what both Jewish history and Jewish jokes reveal is not dissimilar: there's always another way of seeing things, always another place to lay the emphasis, and always another future to look towards – so expect the unexpected!

HOW DO YOU TELL THE DIFFERENCE BETWEEN A GOOD DEAL AND A BAD DEAL?

In the domain of the Jewish joke, you can find beneficiaries of this 'double vision' everywhere:

Mr and Mrs Horowitz are in a restaurant, having soup. Across the room an elegant young woman grins and waves at Mr Horowitz. He tries to shrug it off.

Mrs Horowitz: 'Manny! Who is dat voman?'

Mr Horowitz: 'Dat's ... I'm afraid dat's mine paramour.'

Mrs Horowitz is shocked. After a moment, she asks,

'And who is da other voman vith her?'

Mr Horowitz: 'Dat? Dat's Klein's paramour.'

Mrs Horowitz thinks for a moment: '*Ours* is better.'

While the same historical forces that have taught Mrs Horowitz how to make the best out of a raw deal have also taught Moshe how to query the deal's terms:

Moshe walks into a post office to send a package, but the package is too heavy.

'You'll need another stamp.'

'And *that* should make it lighter?'

Since some things are non-negotiable, however ('money is better than poverty, if only for financial reasons' – Woody Allen), it's fortunate that Jews should happen to be so awfully good at business:

A young Jewish boy starts attending public school in a small town. On day one the teacher asks the class, 'Who was the greatest man that ever lived?'

A girl raises her hand and says, 'Was it Winston Churchill?'

'A good answer,' says the teacher, 'but not the answer I'm looking for.'

Another young student raises her hand and says, 'Was it Shakespeare?'

'Still not the answer I had in mind,' says the teacher.

Then the new Jewish boy raises his hand and says, 'I think Jesus Christ was the greatest man that ever lived.'

The teacher is astonished. 'Yes!' she says. 'That's the answer I was looking for.' She invites him to the front of the class and gives him a lollipop.

Later another Jewish pupil asks him, 'Why did you say "Jesus Christ"?'

The boy replies, 'Look, I know it's Moses, and YOU know it's Moses, but business is business.'

Meanwhile, in the Jewish school, the Hebrew teacher used to boast:

'If I were Rothschild I would be richer than Rothschild.'

'Why?'

'Because *I* would teach Hebrew on the side.'

Not everyone, however, is so easily impressed:

'Mummy I saved money today!'

'How?'

'Instead of buying a ticket to take the bus home, I ran after it all the way!'

'You couldn't have run after a taxi?'

A good deal is just a case of being in the right place at the right time with the right equipment:

Two members of a congregation are talking.

'Our cantor is magnificent,' says the first.

'What's the big deal?' says the second. 'If I had his voice, I'd sing just as well.'

And sometimes *without* the right equipment:

'How much is this pickle?'

'A nickel.'

'But the stall down the street sells them for just three cents!'

'So why don't you buy there?'

'Cos he's run out of pickles.'

'When I run out of pickles, I also sell them for three cents.'

Still, everyone feels there's one deal that escaped them:

Maurice, a young Jew, comes to north London and applies for a job as caretaker at the Edgware

Synagogue. The synagogue committee are just about to offer him the job when they discover that he is illiterate. They decide for many reasons that it would be inappropriate to have an illiterate caretaker. So Maurice leaves and decides to forge a career in another business. He chooses to sell plastic goods door to door. He does well and soon is able to buy a car and, later, to open a store, and then a second and a third. Finally he is ready to open a vast chain of stores and so applies to the underwriter for insurance. But when the underwriter asks him to sign the contract it becomes obvious he cannot write. Shocked to discover that such a successful man has no education, the bank manager says, 'Just think what you could have been if you had learned to read and write.'

'Yes,' says Maurice regretfully, 'caretaker at Edgware synagogue.'

But if Mrs Horowitz and the chain-store owner have learned how to succeed by adopting bourgeois values under capitalist conditions, Jews have also had to manage the art of the deal under communist ones:

One winter in Soviet Moscow, the rumour went around that a meat delivery had arrived from the collective farm. Real sausage! Within minutes, a vast queue wound around Peshkov the butcher's, like an anaconda around a cow. But after an hour, the manager came out and announced, 'Comrades, there is less meat than we thought. Can all the Jews leave.'

Out go the Jews. Two hours later, the manager faces the crowd again: 'I'm afraid there's even less than we thought – only enough for Party members.'

Half the crowd shuffles off. An hour later: 'There really is very little meat. Anyone who didn't fight in the October Revolution must go.'

Now just two old men are left. Three hours later, as darkness falls, the manager emerges: 'Comrades, there will be no sausage after all today.'

'You see,' says one old man to the other, 'The Jews get the best deal.'

(No wonder Jews have a reputation for double-dealing.)

HOW DO YOU TELL THE DIFFERENCE BETWEEN A TAILOR AND A PSYCHIATRIST?

A deal is a deal is a deal, and you have to deal with whatever hand you're dealt. That means, in the first place, being adaptable. And one advantage to Jews of having learned to expect the unexpected is that they've acquired just that skill: the ability to change just enough to meet the latest terms and conditions.[*]

As too have their jokes. Thus whether it's Capitalist America or Soviet Russia, the same old jokes should always be framed in terms of the current polity:

---

[*] According to the historian Yuri Slezkine, it's their talent for adapting that rendered Jews modern people *avant la lettre*: 'Modernisation is about everyone becoming urban, mobile, literate, articulate, intellectually intricate, physically fastidious and occupationally flexible.' (Not to mention witty.)

Back in the shtetl, Moishe got a job looking out for signs of the coming of the Messiah: 'It's a boring job, and the pay's terrible – but at least it's steady work.'

While in the Soviet era his job changed: Moishe now found himself looking out for signs of world revolution. The job proved equally steady.

Which I guess you could say is the *other* message we get from both the Jewish joke and Jewish history: expect the unexpected for sure, but also – expect more of the same. For as earnestly as they may long for the Messiah, Jews are also a people who've learned to pray: 'Lord, don't let this war last as long as we're able to survive it.' And so, since they've grown a bit weary of big-time historical promises, what you often find in Jewish jokes is a capacity for looking past the popular ideology of the moment towards the brute material reality running beneath:

'By the year 2000 Russians will be able to get a rocket to Mars,' declared Brezhnev.

'And when,' asks Mendel, 'will we be able to get to Vienna?'

Mendel's real wish, though, is to travel overseas – to America:

> He goes to get a visa. 'There's a long, long queue for those,' he's told by the official, 'you'd best come back in another ten years.'

> 'Fine,' says Mendel, 'in the morning or the afternoon?'

Mendel's patience, in fact, is not unlike that of the Jewish joke, whose very endurance is a testament to its critical powers. For if the joke's *still got it*, then the new ideology, no matter how different or how radical, can't be quite so transformative as advertised. So while some of the best Jewish jokes *have* been put out of action by recent transformations – email, for example, has called time on the traditional Jewish telegram:

> Start worrying. Details to follow.

Still, the sentiment remains the same: if you start worrying now, history will be sure to prove you right.

But never forget the flipside, that what goes around comes around:

A Jewish couple are wheeling their baby boy in a pram. A woman peeks in and says, 'What a sweet child! What's his name?' 'Shloyme.' 'Shloyme! What kind of name is that?' 'We named him after his grandfather, Scott.'*

Thus lots of Jewish jokes have kept pace with modernity not only because Jews have been sceptical about historical change, but because they've also been so very good at it:

Q: What's the difference between a tailor and a psychiatrist?

A: A generation.

* This one's very much an insiders' joke alluding to changing fashions in Jewish assimilation: whereas early generations of Jewish immigrants tended to Americanize their names by translating Yiddish or Hebrew names into English near equivalents, in recent years there has been a trend for young hipster Jews to select the sort of names their great-grandparents might have had.

HOW DO YOU TELL THE DIFFERENCE BETWEEN MORALITY AND NEUROSIS?*

Here, on the other hand, is what distinguishes a *physician* from a psychiatrist:

> A psychiatrist is a Jewish physician who can't stand the sight of blood.

Jewish history, after all, has not only seen a lot of blood, it's also seen a lot of psychology.

And for Freud, of course, jokes, alongside dreams and verbal slips, are a way *in* to the unofficial part of oneself he called the unconscious. So do Jewish jokes

---

* If only I knew. Freud's entire life's work was arguably an attempt to tell this difference.

provide evidence of the *Jewish* unconscious? If so, the Jewish joke might then be supposed to remember what other archives of Jewish life have sought to forget. Starting with this joke:

> What's the definition of Jewish Alzheimer's? You forget everything but the guilt.

Oh boy, the guilt! What a Gordian knot of an emotion that is. Jews might *well* forget everything but the guilt – because guilt attests to a history that you can deny all you like, but it's still got its hands around your neck.

But while our guilt likes to remind us that there's something in our past that needs dealing with, it tends not to be too straightforward about what that something is. Guilt is a feeling that hides as much as it reveals, and it's a feeling that works to repress other feelings: aggressive feelings, for example, or incestuous ones. So you could say that guilt, too, is a bit of a joke. Hence why Maureen Lipman's revision of the joke – 'Jewish Alzheimer's is forgetting everything except a grudge' – is just as funny and equally revealing. For both guilt *and* jokes are socially sanctioned ways of masking our unconscious intentions towards those we feel guilty about, or feel inclined to joke about (albeit by finding an outward outlet for its forbidden feelings, joking is generally the healthier of the two). Might that, then, explain why there are so many Jewish jokes *about* Jewish guilt?

We're back to those Jewish mothers sitting in the dark. And when it comes to pinning guilt on the Jewish mother, Jewish jokes can get *very* dark. See for instance the most lightbulb-less example of a Jewish mother joke in Philip Roth's novel-length send-up of the Jewish mother, *Portnoy's Complaint* (1969). It features a neighbourhood kid whose suicide note reads:

> Mrs Blumenthal called. Please bring your mah-jongg rules to the game tonight.
>
> Ronald

No matter the fallout, though, you should know that the Jewish mother does have a method to her madness:

> Let your son hear you sigh every day. If you don't know what he's done to make you sigh, *he* will.

And, to be fair to her, guilt is a symptom from which she too suffers:

> When the Jewish mother was called up for jury service, they had to send her home because she kept on insisting *she* was guilty.

So it's only reasonable if she passes it on to her friends:

> The afternoon is drawing to a close, and the guests are getting ready to leave.
>
> 'Mrs Goldberg,' says one of the ladies. 'I just wanted to tell you that your cookies were so delicious I ate four of them.'
>
> 'You ate five,' replies Mrs Goldberg. 'But who's counting?'

And to her family:

> The Jewish mother, upon receiving a phone call from her adult daughter, announces: 'I'm very weak, I'm starving, I haven't eaten for two weeks'

'Why ever not, Mother?!'

'Because I didn't want that I should have my mouth full when you rang.'

HOW DO YOU TELL THE DIFFERENCE BETWEEN A JEWISH WOMAN AND A SHIKSA?

Of course, the Jewish mother also has plenty to say when it's someone else who's starving:

> Once, a homeless woman accosted her on the street:
>
> 'Miss, I haven't eaten in three days.'
>
> 'Force yourself', she replied.

If 'let them eat cake' is the mistake that too much money can make, 'force yourself' is an error of too much analysis:

Sadie Goldberg wants to expand her intellectual horizons, so she goes to a lecture on 'Human Sexuality' by the eminent psychoanalyst Dr Feigenbaum.

She is so entranced that at the end of the lecture she decides to approach him.

'Dr Feigenbaum,' she says, 'I want you to know I found your lecture fascinating. There was just one thing I didn't quite get. You kept referring to "bestiality". What is that?'

'OK,' Feigenbaum says, 'so bestiality is the practice of a human being having relations with an animal. For example, you may wanna have sex with a dog.'

'A dog?!'

'Yeah, a dog. Or you may wanna have sex with … a horse.'

'A *horse*?!?!'

'Yeah, a horse. Or you may wanna have sex with a bull.'

'A BULL???!!!!?!!'

'Yeah, a bull, or maybe you wanna have sex with a chicken?'

'A chicken? Feh ...'

But though Sadie Goldberg may fancy a bull, the husband of a Jewish woman will get no action if he compares her to a cow:

An impoverished couple in a poor shtetl in Poland couldn't make a living on their farm so they asked their neighbour what to to. 'You must buy a cow, feed it up, and then when it is ready take it to a bull. When she mates, you will have a calf, the calf will grow up and then you have two cows.' This is the way to riches. So they saved and saved and saved until they could afford to buy a cow. Then they fattened her up and took her to the bull. However, whenever the bull came close to the cow, the cow would move away.

The couple were frantic; they decided to ask the rabbi what to do. They told the rabbi what was happening: 'Whenever the bull approaches our cow, she moves away. If he approaches from the back, she moves forward. When he approaches her from the front, she backs off. An approach from the side and she just walks away to the other side.'

The rabbi thought about this for a minute and asked, 'Did you buy this cow from Minsk?'

The people were dumbfounded. 'You are truly a wise rabbi,' they said. 'How did you know we got the cow from Minsk?'

The rabbi answered sadly, 'My vife, she is from Minsk.'

Winning the heart of a Jewish woman is thus a complex and subtle art:

Heschel was in awe of his friend Abe. Abe could get any woman he wanted – and he did. 'Teach me how you do it,' Heschel begged him.

'It's easy,' said Abe, 'the trick with attracting Jewish women is that you have to show them you care about three things: food, family and philosophy. Food, because that means you care about their physical well-being. Family, because that means your intentions are serious. Philosophy, because that means you respect their intelligence.'

Heschel was thankful for the advice and asked a woman he fancied on a date. 'Tell me,' he opened, 'do you like to eat kugel [baked noodle pudding]?'

'I can't stand kugel,' his date replied.

'Hmm, so does your brother eat kugel?' he tried again.

'I don't have a brother,' she retorted.

'I see,' Heschel pressed on, 'And tell me, if you *did* have a brother, do you think he would like kugel?'

But philosophy isn't only useful when dating – it has its place in the bedroom too:

Shmuley returns home to find clothes strewn everywhere, and his wife undressed in bed, tying up her hair. Feeling suspicious, he starts frantically searching around until at last he finds his old foe Itzhik hiding in the cupboard.

'Vhat,' Shmuley splutters, 'are *you* doing here?'

'Everyone,' Itzhik replies, 'has got to be somewhere.'

He's got a point. Though Itzhik's philosophical defence might at root be considered an historical one if we recall all those out-of-place Jews who were forced, under somewhat different circumstances, to use much the same defence when faced by interrogators far more fearsome than Shmuley.

But never mind Abe and Heschel or Shmuley and Itzhik. We're talking here of the Jewish woman, and of what Jewish jokes tell us about *her*. And what they tell us, for one thing, is that she adheres to neither side of patriarchy's most enduring binary – the virgin/the whore – but admits instead of another stereotype: a stereotype that's still sexist, but at least she makes it her own.

Because you *can* get a Jewish woman into bed, it's just that she doesn't make it easy for you. And besides, she's always dealing with a million other things at the same time:

Three old men are discussing their sex lives.

The Italian says, 'Last week, my wife and I had great sex. I rubbed her body all over with olive oil, we made passionate love, and she screamed for five minutes at the end.'

The Frenchman boasts, 'Last week when my wife and I had sex, I rubbed her body all over with butter. We then made passionate love and she screamed for fifteen minutes.'

The Jewish man says, 'Last week, my wife and I had sex. I rubbed her body all over with chicken fat, we made love, and she screamed for six hours.'

The others are stunned and ask, 'What could you have possibly done to make your wife scream for six hours?'

'I wiped my hands on the curtains.'

Since sex in Jewish law *is* considered a mitzvah (good deed), however, even a very orthodox Jewish woman can find reasons to enjoy it:

A nineteen-year-old religious boy marries an eighteen-year-old religious girl. Both are sexual innocents before their wedding. After the wedding ceremony and celebration is over they go home and do the mitzvah. On the second night after they're married, he says to her, 'You know, I had a grandmother, of blessed memory, who raised me like a son. She couldn't be at our wedding. In memory of her soul we should do the mitzvah again.' Third night he says to her, 'I had a cousin, we were like brothers. He died too young. In his memory we should do the mitzvah again.' And they do. On the fourth night he mentions another cousin. On the fifth night an uncle, then an aunt, and a great-uncle.

Come Shabbat, she gets herself to synagogue. All her friends surround her: 'Nu, what's he like?'

'He's a fool, but I get nachas [pleasure] from the family.'

To find this joke as funny as I do – I find it very funny – you'd need to understand the context: the importance, in orthodox circles, of marrying into a respectable family. For only then can you expect to find yourself laughing aloud at what I take to be the joke's key revelation: that however hard you may try to hide what gets you going under the cover of respectability – such as within the sanctity of a marriage, for instance – still, there's no such thing as an 'innocent pleasure'.

How so?*

To recap, two young, religious and sexually inexperienced people are rather more capable than they might have us believe of following the logic of their own desires. Although, throughout the joke, we're made aware of the groom's use of pious rhetoric to serve his own pleasurable ends, it's the punchline revelation of the bride's polymorphously perverse satisfactions – i.e. the pleasure identified in the joke as 'nachas' is that huge turn-on enjoyed by a Jewish woman who senses she's 'married well' – that really gives the game away. Because, my goodness, here we have a Jewish woman who, no less than the Jewish man, no less than anyone in fact, is her own brand of pervert! She gets her pleasure, that is, from the feeling that there's something more to be enjoyed, something beyond or beside what she's been officially given. Thus her sexual pleasure is not unlike the pleasure *we* get from the joke: the pleasure of secrecy, of doubleness, of a double entendre. So

---

* One benefit of including an abstruse joke fewer readers are liable to get is that the po-faced business of then explaining and interpreting the joke should feel a bit less ruinous.

79

it's a joke, in other words, whose comic disturbance of its protagonists' presumed innocence perfectly illustrates what delights and disturbs us all in that everyday form of taboo-breaking we try to pass off as nothing really, as an innocent pleasure – as only joking.

What's critical, then, is that, no matter how she gets her kicks, this young woman's piety remains unimpeachable. She does nothing overtly transgressive. On the contrary, she's doing her duty – her conjugal duty. As such, she's hard put to explain the sex – or the pleasure – that *isn't* a mitzvah:

> Becky returns home and finds her husband in bed with her best friend. Shocked, she rounds on her friend: 'Me – I have to, but *you*?'

Truly, the bedroom is full of philosophy.

But if the Jewish woman typically needs to be talked into bed, shiksas, we're assured, are always up for it:

> A rabbi and a beautiful model get stuck in a lift. The model turns to the rabbi and says, 'Before we press the alarm ... I have to confess, I, I, I ... always

fantasised about having sex with a rabbi. Why don't we take this opportunity?'

The rabbi thinks about it for a moment and then asks, 'What's in it for me?'

And they're endlessly obliging:

A congregation honours a rabbi for twenty-five years of service by sending him on holiday to Hawaii, all expenses paid.

When the rabbi walks into his room, there's a gorgeous woman lying naked on the bed. She tells the rabbi that she is here for him at any time during his trip. Naturally, the rabbi is shocked and extremely embarrassed. Who has dared to imagine that he would even *want* such a thing?

The woman tells him who is paying for her services. He picks up the phone, calls the synagogue, and asks for the president of the congregation: 'Where is your respect, how could you do something like this? Have I ever done anything to suggest that I'm the type of person to appreciate this sort of "gift"? As your rabbi, I am very hurt, and very angry.'

As he continues to berate the president, the woman gets up and starts to get dressed, not wanting to embarrass the rabbi any more than necessary.

The rabbi turns to her and says, 'Where are you going? I'm not angry at *you*.'

I love that joke, but who is it a joke 'on' exactly? Am I laughing along with an anti-Semitic slur – an essentially racist joke about hypocritical Jews? Or is the joke a subtler but still rather anti-Semitic indictment of the sophistry of *religious* Jews specifically? Or maybe it's a joke about not Jews so much as men – as in *all* men, including rabbis? Unless, that is, it's a joke on each and every one of us – a joke about the self-justifying manoeuvres that one can always discern between the lines of just about *any* system of public morality. (Though that it's a rabbi who teaches us this moral lesson – a moral lesson about the immorality of morality – does make it that bit funnier):

A rabbi who's been leading a congregation for many years is upset by the fact that he's never been able to eat pork. So he devises a plan whereby he flies to a remote tropical island and checks into a hotel. He immediately gets himself a table at the finest restaurant and orders the most expensive pork dish on the menu, a whole suckling pig.

As he's eagerly waiting for it to be served, he hears his name called from across the restaurant. He looks up to see ten of his loyal congregants approaching. His luck, they'd chosen the same time to visit the same remote location!

Just at that moment, the waiter comes out with a huge silver tray carrying a whole roasted pig complete with an apple in its mouth. The rabbi looks up sheepishly at his congregants and says, 'Wow – you order an apple in this place and look how it's served!'

Well, at least it makes a change from man's standard calumny of blaming his *own* hankering for forbidden apples on a woman.

And not just any woman …

HOW DO YOU TELL THE DIFFERENCE BETWEEN A JEWISH MOTHER AND A JEWISH MOTHER-IN-LAW?

Here's how:

Goldie and Frieda were chatting. Goldie says, 'So nu, how's your daughter?'

Frieda responds, 'Oh, just fine. My daughter is married to the most wonderful man. She never has to cook, he always takes her out. She never has to clean, he got her a housekeeper. She never has to work, he's got such a good job. She never has to worry about the children, he got her a nanny.'

Then Goldie asks, 'And how is your son these days?'

Frieda says, 'Just awful. He is married to such a witch
of a woman. She makes him take her out to dinner
every night, she never cooks a dish. She made him get
her a housekeeper, God forbid she should vacuum a
carpet! He has to work like a dog because she won't
get a job, and she never takes care of their children,
because she made him get her a nanny!'

Ouch.

But let's deal with the mother-in-law first:

A Jewish town had a shortage of men for wedding
purposes, so they tried to import men from other
towns. Finally a groom-to-be arrived on a train, and
two mothers-in-law-to-be awaited him, each claiming true ownership.

A rabbi was called to solve the problem. After a few
minutes of thought, he said, 'If this is the situation,
you both claim the groom, we'll cut him in half and
give each one of you half of him.'

To this replied one woman, 'If that's the case, fine,
give him to the other woman.'

The rabbi intoned wisely, 'So be it. The one willing to cut him in half, *that* has to be the real mother-in-law!'

Thus, while a father-in-law can sometimes disguise his true feelings …

A girl brings her new boyfriend, a serious young scholar studying Torah, home to meet her father. The father takes the boy into his study and begins to ask him questions.

'So,' says the father, 'you're a Torah scholar. How do you plan to support my daughter?'

'Don't worry,' says the boy, 'God will provide.'

'And where will the two of you live?' asks the father.

'Don't worry, God will provide.'

'And how will you support your children?'

'Don't worry,' says the boy, 'God will provide.'

The father finishes his discussion and the young man leaves. The daughter then comes in and asks her father, 'So, what did you think of him?'

'I like him,' says the father. 'He thinks I'm God.'

... a mother-in-law will always let you know what she thinks:

Jake visited his parents. He said, 'Finally, I've found my true love. Just for fun, I'm going to bring over three women and you can guess which one she is.'

The next day he brought three beautiful women, who sat on the sofa and chatted with his parents over a little cake. After they left, he challenged, 'OK, guess which one I'm going to marry?'

'The one in the middle with the red hair,' his mother replied instantly.

'Right! But ... how did you know?' asked Jake, amazed.

'Simple,' his mother said. '*Her*, we don't like.'

Which doesn't mean she won't get as good as she gives:

Sadie is dying. As she lies on her deathbed, she says to her husband, 'Shlomo, I want you to promise me one thing.'

'Anything darling,' says Shlomo.

'On the day of my funeral I want you to look after my mother. And you and she must travel there together in the same car,' says Sadie.

Shlomo squirms. He struggles. At last he says, 'For you, on your funeral, I will do this. But let me tell you right now – it will *completely* ruin the day for me.'

When it comes to his *own* mother, though, a Jewish man sees things rather differently:

Hymie is beside himself – his wife is in bed and it's clear she's dying. Nothing will revive her – not water, not whisky, not food of any kind. 'Is there *anything* I can do to bring you joy in your last moments?' he pleads.

'Well, there is one thing,' she replies, 'I'd like to have intercourse with you, Hymie, one last time.'

Hymie obliges. Miraculously, his wife is completely revivified by their coupling. She's not only better, she's better than ever. She leaps out of bed, ready for anything. Hymie, seeing this, bursts into tears.

'Whatever's wrong, my Hymie?' she asks. 'Aren't you pleased to see me so well? We'll have many more happy years together.'

'It's not that,' sobs Hymie, 'it's just got me thinking – *I could have saved Mother!*'

So the Jewish joke, then, has a theory of neurotic guilt that both extends and revises the one we've inherited from Freud; for, as we find it here, what the Jewish son feels most guilty about is precisely his *failure* to be incestuous (which theory, personally, I think has some mileage).

Ah, but Oedipus Shmedipus, as long as he loves his mother:

Mother 1: My son loves me so much – he constantly buys me gifts.

Mother 2: My son loves me so much – he always takes me on holiday.

Jewish Mother: That's nothing. My son loves me so much, he goes to see a special doctor five times a week to talk exclusively about me.

So we must pity the Jewish mother! Sometimes it seems as if the entire Jewish joking industry exists only in order to poke fun at her: narcissistic, self-martyring, smothering, guilt-inducing, hysterical, paranoid, overweening, complaining, castrating – honestly, is there any sin she *hasn't* been accused of by her ungrateful children?

Her daughter certainly expects the world of her:

Mitzy springs to the telephone when it rings and listens with relief to the kindly voice in her ear.

'How are you, darling?' it asks. 'What kind of a day are you having?'

'Oh, Mother,' she says, breaking into bitter tears, 'I've had such a bad day. The baby won't eat and the washing machine broke down. I haven't had a chance to go shopping, and besides, I've just sprained my ankle and I have to hobble around. On top of that, the house is a mess and I'm supposed to have two couples to dinner tonight.'

The mother is shocked and is at once all sympathy. 'Oh, darling,' she says, 'sit down, relax and close your eyes. I'll be over in half an hour. I'll do your shopping, clean up the house and cook your dinner for you. I'll feed the baby and I'll call a repairman to fix the washing machine. Now stop crying. I'll do everything. In fact, I'll even call Simon at the office and tell him he ought to come home and help out for once.'

'Simon?' says Mitzy. 'Who's Simon?'

'Why, Simon! Your husband!'

'No it isn't. I'm married to Shlomo.'

'Oh, I'm sorry. I guess I have the wrong number.'

There's a short pause before Mitzy says, 'Does this mean you're *not* coming over?'

But when it comes to mother-blaming, it's really the Jewish mother's ultimate victim, her poor emasculated son, who is the first to point the finger and cry '*J'accuse*'. He, after all, is famously the object of such mountainous maternal pride that she can't even stop herself boasting about him when he's in mortal danger:

'Help! Help! My son – a doctor! – is drowning!'

Though her maternal narcissism took root much earlier, of course:

Mrs Cohen is pleased to announce the birth of her son, Dr David Cohen.

The announcement may *sound* premature, but you have to remember at which moment life is said to begin in Jewish tradition:

In Jewish tradition the foetus is not considered a viable human being until after graduation from medical school.

And actually Mrs Cohen predicted Instagram too:

When pushing David along in his buggy one day, she bumps into Mrs Shindler.

'Oh, what a beautiful baby!' Mrs Shindler coos.

'Meh, that's nothing,' replies Mrs Cohen, 'you should see his photos.'

But that's what you get in a culture that puts family first:

Ninety-one-year-old Morris and Sophie, his eighty-nine-year-old wife of sixty-six years, go to their lawyer to get a divorce. Puzzled, the lawyer asks, 'Why did you wait all this time if you were both so miserable for so long?'

Sophie replies, 'We were waiting for the children to die.'

And a culture that will do whatever it takes to keep loved ones close:

Goldie Cohen, an elderly Jewish lady from New York, goes to her travel agent. 'I vont to go to India.'

'Mrs Cohen, why India? It's filthy, and much hotter than New York.'

'I vont to go to India.'

'But it's a long journey, and those trains, how will you manage? What will you eat? The food is too hot and spicy for you. You can't drink the water. You must not eat fresh fruit and vegetables. You'll get sick: the plague, hepatitis, cholera, typhoid, malaria, God only knows. What will you do? Can you imagine the hospital, no Jewish doctors? Why torture yourself?'

'I vont to go to India.'

The necessary arrangements are made, and off she goes. She arrives in India and, undeterred by the noise, smell and crowds, makes her way to an ashram. There she joins the seemingly never-ending queue of people waiting for an audience with the guru. An aide tells her that it will take at least three days of standing in line to see the guru.

'Dat's OK.'

Eventually she reaches the hallowed portals. There she is told firmly that she can only say three words.

'Fine.'

She is ushered into the inner sanctum, where the wise guru is seated, ready to bestow spiritual blessings upon eager initiates. Just before she reaches the holy of holies she is once again reminded: 'Remember, just three words.'

Unlike the other devotees, she does not prostrate herself at his feet. She stands directly in front of him, crosses her arms over her chest, fixes her gaze on his and says: 'Sheldon, come home."

So while the Jewish mother can be overprotective:

What's a Jewish sweater? The woollen garment worn by a child when his mother is cold.

That's only because she doesn't like to see him sitting around like a guru all day doing nothing useful. On the contrary, she's ambitious for him:

A little Jewish boy is telling his mother about how he's won a part in a play at school. His mother asks, 'What is the part you will play, Saul?' Saul responds,

---

* Whenever I hear that joke it's always with the name Sheldon in the punchline, which dates the joke (taking it back to the countercultural trends in America in the 1950s and 1960s), but also makes the joke impossible to update: no other name seems as funny or works as well.

'I shall play the Jewish husband,' to which the mother replies, 'Pah! Well, you go right back to that teacher and tell her that you want a SPEAKING part!'

Hang on! Is it *really* the woman who gets such a great speaking part in all these Jewish jokes? Or aren't these jokes mostly told by men precisely in order to pin the blame for their own guilt – or their own Jewishness – on a woman? And, as we know, it was Adam, the first man, who paved the way here, by blaming his own tsores on Eve, the first woman.

Adam started a trend. For who, in any man's life, *is* the first woman if not his mother: a woman so spectacularly powerful that he entered the world wholly on her account, and then relied on her for his own survival? So it's having a mother at all that's emasculating. And that goes double for Jewish men – and especially Jewish men from first-generation immigrant families who tended to wield less power in the world than Gentile men, rendering them subject to more domesticity and more mothering. Hence, though to some extent *all* the jokes Jewish men tell about Jewish women seem really to be jokes about the overwhelming influence of their mothers, the merciless mother-bashing of the male Jewish stand-up act during its 1950s and 1960s heyday should be seen in the context of a distinct historical backdrop.

That said, the most notorious comic creation of the Jewish mother stereotype belongs to neither biblical patriarch nor secular stand-up, but comes to us instead from a novelist. It's Philip Roth's 'most unforgettable character', Sophie Portnoy, who is the guilt-inducing Jewish mother par excellence.* As Alex, her long-suffering son, complains:

> The legend engraved on the face of the Jewish nickel – on the body of every Jewish child! – not IN GOD WE TRUST, but SOMEDAY YOU'LL BE A PARENT AND YOU'LL KNOW WHAT IT'S LIKE.

And the novel comprises exclusively Alex's monologue as he lies on his back on a psychiatrist's couch, tirelessly complaining about the damage inflicted on him by his mother's fantasised omnipotence:

> It's a family joke that when I was a tiny child I turned from the window out of which I was watching a

---

* Roth entitles the first section of the novel, about Sophie, 'The Most Unforgettable Character I've Met'.

snowstorm, and hopefully asked, 'Momma, do we believe in winter?'

If a Freudian slip is when you say one thing but mean your mother, then every joke is a 'family joke'.

HOW DO YOU TELL THE DIFFERENCE BETWEEN A MALE JEWISH COMEDIAN AND A FEMALE JEWISH COMEDIAN?

Alexander Portnoy complains that 'I am the son in the Jewish joke – only it ain't no joke!' But it's Sophie – the target not only of the Jewish joke's internalised anti-Semitism, but of a large dose of misogyny as well – who can really be found drowning in the Jewish joke. So who will rescue *her*, another writer, Grace Paley, asks, from 'her son the doctor and her son the novelist'?

Why, the female joker, of course!*

---

* At least, when she isn't self-harming or being taken to task for doing so. Alluding to fellow Jewish 'funny girl' Fanny Brice's rhinoplasty in 1923, Dorothy Parker quipped that Brice had 'cut off her nose to spite her race.'

Yet there's a nasty rumour abroad, you hear it again and again: women just aren't as funny as men. To which you always want to reply: well, they try not to laugh in your face maybe. For women in public *are* much more bound by the conventions of civility – of having to please everyone all the time – that can make poking fun a riskier business for them. This was something that the late Joan Rivers, perhaps the most caustic of female comics, understood only too well. 'One of the most rebellious things a woman can do,' she once said, 'is allow people to think she's mean.' The mere fact, in other words, of a woman going public with her funniness can throw a certain light on the degree to which a misogynist culture has turned comedy – including Jewish comedy – into an ultra-defensive boys' club.

Not that it's so hard sending up the boys:

My ancestors wandered lost in the wilderness for forty years because even in biblical times, men would not stop to ask for directions. *Elayne Boosler*

Most men are secretly still mad at their mothers for throwing away their comic books. They would be valuable now. *Rita Rudner*

My mother always said don't marry for money. Divorce for money. *Wendy Liebman*

I don't have any kids. Well, at least none I know about. *Cathy Ladman*

But female comedians do more than simply deliver low blows where they know it hurts. They also use their acts to critique the stratagems of male-centric comedy. When, that is, we hear men's jokes told *by* women, we cannot but hear them differently – hence why that line from Cathy Ladman, which word for word parrots a stereotypically male comedy brag, is about as deft a moment of comic outwitting as you could wish for.

And the same logic goes doubly when women tell jokes about areas of female experience that no male comic should reasonably expect to get away with. Here, for instance, is Sarah Silverman:

I was raped by a doctor, which is so bittersweet for a Jewish girl.

To my ears, there's a world of difference between this and a male-authored 'rape joke', but not everyone believes that gender does anything to justify such a gag. And that, in a nutshell, is the trouble for the comedian – and especially the female comedian, whose use of obscenity or brashness always sparks greater outrage – there are those who will be scandalised by pretty much every joke she tells. Hence the advice of Joan Rivers: 'We don't apologise for a joke. We are comics. We are here to make you laugh. If you don't get it, then don't watch us.'

Such advice can only be inspirational for Sarah Silverman. Because it's true, Silverman's Jewish jokes *have* upset certain Jews, and her rape jokes *have* upset certain women – including certain Jewish women* – and it's true too that Silverman has stood accused, as Philip Roth was in the 1960s, of self-hatred. So with an act like Silverman's we can find, once again, the same old questions getting asked: is such comedy needlessly offensive? Is it, all told, even witty? And is it, ultimately, defensible or indefensible?

And, as ever, context is everything: it always depends on who is telling the joke, who is hearing it, and to what end. Roth, for instance, has assured us that he has yet to receive a letter of thanks from an anti-Semitic organisation. And so far as I'm aware, misogynists haven't written to thank Silverman for her great services to their cause either. So while it's

---

* 'Put me up against Sarah Silverman and I could take her' *Joan Rivers*.

important to be mindful of sensitivities, it's just as important to remain wary of the humour police, those punchline vigilantes who so often wind up silencing the very people they're claiming to defend. For though, in the majority of situations, humour is seldom the only answer, and by no means always the best one, what humourlessness always fails to recognise is just how *useful* a sense of humour can be for confronting what one finds offensive, including offensive jokes – as can be seen from the long tradition of comedians wrong-footing their abusers by making the mud slung their way a valuable commodity: material they can *work* with.

Take, for example, another young Jewish American comedian, Amy Schumer, who sparked the predictable yowls of outrage after tweeting this image of herself:

And who then doubled the 'offence' by parodying the demand for an apology in her follow-up tweet:

.@amyschumer my bad. I meant to say "A Jew with 2 horns"

RETWEETS 26   LIKES 490

1:32 PM - 2 Mar 2016

Some allege that such quips see Schumer reinforcing the ugly stereotyping of Jews throughout their history. But can't we regard them instead as an intervention *into* that history? Because what we find with playfulness like Schumer's is not anti-Semitism, surely, but quite the opposite: a seriously funny Jewish woman taking on history *by* the horns.

HOW DO YOU TELL THE DIFFERENCE BETWEEN A KING AND A BEGGAR?

Ever since the first ape slipped on the first banana skin, a sense of humour has assumed a sense of the slippery: a sense with which one can not only find the funny *in* the joke, but one can transform what's funny *about* the joke.

The Jewish joke is a case in point. The debate over whether Jewish jokes are battling anti-Semitism or are in fact forms of it isn't anything so new. Back in the bad old days, for example, there was clearly an anti-Semitic way of interpreting the joke about the Jew who, upon finding his fellow passenger is also Jewish, instantly puts his feet up on the seat in front of him ('You see! Jews among themselves reveal who they *really* are ... dirty and uncivilised!'). And yet precisely here is where that most famous promoter of the slip – Sigmund Freud – identified something else: the democratic spirit of a people who will brook no hierarchy, because all, ultimately, are members of the same human family.*

We see this no better than in the typical Jewish beggar/shnorrer joke. In the oral storytelling of the Hasidim, the shnorrer in the parable invariably turns out to be a king (or an angel) in disguise. But in the Jewish joke it's the other way around, as *now* it's the nobleman who winds up exasperatedly begging:

> A shnorrer tries without success to get an appointment with Rothschild. Finally he stands outside the family mansion and shouts, 'My family is starving to death and the baron refuses to see me!'
>
> Rothschild acquiesces and gives the shnorrer thirty rubles. 'Here you are,' he says. 'And let me tell you that if you hadn't caused such a scene, I would have given you sixty rubles.'
>
> 'My dear Baron,' replies the shnorrer, 'I don't tell you how to conduct your business, so you don't tell me how to conduct mine.'

---

* Especially if you're from a Sephardi family and have been told that pretty much everyone you meet is related to you – you're just never quite sure how.

* * *

In Rome, two beggars are sitting on the ground, a few feet apart. One wears a large cross. The other, a Star of David. Needless to say, the plate of the former fills up quickly, with almost nothing in the plate of the latter.

After some time, a kindly priest passes and sizes up the situation. He turns to the Jewish beggar: 'My son, you should put away that Star of David. You will never make enough money wearing that.'

After he leaves, the Jewish beggar turns to the other with an annoyed look: 'Could you believe that guy, telling the Goldberg brothers how to run their business?'

* * *

The shnorrer begged the baron for some money for a journey to Ostend; his doctor had recommended sea-bathing for his troubles. The baron thought Ostend was a particularly expensive resort; wouldn't a cheaper one do equally well? The shnorrer disagreed. 'Herr Baron,' he said, 'I consider nothing too expensive for my health.'

* * *

A poor and desperate man borrowed £100 from a rich acquaintance. The very same day his benefactor met him again in a restaurant with a plate of caviar in front of him.

'What? You borrow money from me and then order yourself caviar? Is that what you've used my money for?'

'I don't understand you,' replied the poor man. 'If I haven't any money I can't eat caviar, and if I have some money then I mustn't eat caviar. Then, when can I eat caviar?'

* * *

A shnorrer, allowed as a needy guest into a wealthy man's house every Sabbath, one day brings an unknown young man with him and sits down to eat.

'Who is this?' asked the householder.

'He's my new son-in-law,' the shnorrer replied. 'I've promised him his board for the first year.'

* * *

Chernov, the shnorrer of Petrograd, had a very wealthy patron who, for some obscure reason, had taken a liking to the nervy little beggar. Each year he would give Chernov a handsome stipend – never less than five hundred rubles. One year, however, the rich man gave him only two hundred and fifty rubles.

'What is the meaning of this?' demanded the insolent shnorrer. 'This is only half of what you have been giving me!'

'I'm sorry, Chernov, but I must cut my expenses this year,' apologised the wealthy man. 'My son married an actress and I am paying all the bills.'

'Well, of all the chutzpah!' roared Chernov, hopping mad. 'If your son wants to support an actress, that's his business. But how dare he do it with my money!'

Thinking of the Jewish concept of tzedakah – a form of charity that equates to social justice – Freud says: 'The truth that lies behind is that the schnorrer, who in his thoughts treats the rich man's money as his own, has actually, according to the sacred ordinances of the Jews, almost a right to make this confusion.' So the very same jokes that denigrate Jews in the eyes of some appear as powerful lessons in Jewish ethics in the eyes of others. Though there are of course limits:

A baron, deeply moved by a shnorrer's tale of woe, rang for his servants. 'Throw him out!' he said. 'He's breaking my heart!'

HOW DO YOU TELL THE DIFFERENCE BETWEEN JEWS AND ISRAELIS?

If two Jews alone with each other on the same train feel free to make themselves at home by flouting the rules, then what can we expect of the Jewish State? Can a whole country run on chutzpah?

By the looks of things, yes. In Israel it does appear as if those same overfamiliar manners have prevailed:

As the plane set down at Ben Gurion airport, the voice of the captain came on: 'Please remain seated with your seat belt fastened until this plane is at a complete standstill and the seat-belt signs have been turned off.

'To those who are seated, we wish you a merry Christmas, and hope that you enjoy your stay in

Israel ... and to those of you standing in the aisles and pushing towards the doors, we wish you a happy Hanukkah, and welcome back home.'

Yet there are those who maintain a big difference between diasporic and nationalist personalities. Israelis, says a character in the film *The Infidel* (2010), are 'Jews without angst, without guilt, therefore not really Jews at all'. Or, in other words, what makes Jews recognisably Jewish is their self-consciousness before an audience, which brings them a constant nagging sense of how they might be seen from the outside:

On a bus in Tel Aviv, a mother is talking to her small child in Yiddish. But he keeps answering her in Hebrew. Each time, his mother corrects him: 'No, no, talk Yiddish.'

An increasingly exasperated Israeli, overhearing all of this, demands to know, 'Why do you insist your son speaks Yiddish instead of Hebrew?'

'Because,' the boy's mother replies, 'I don't want him to forget he's a Jew.'

She gets the problem, in other words – if diasporic Jewishness has become a byword for difference, then how can Jewishness be sustained in Israel? The stereotypical splits and tensions to be found within diasporic jokes can hardly be expected to work in a place where the majority are Jews:

A classical musician was performing a solo recital in Israel. As he concluded his performance he was astounded by the cries from the audience: 'Play it again!' He was incredibly moved by this response, and gladly did so. As he finished a second time, he was astonished to hear their demands once more: 'Play it again!'

He bowed to the audience, wiped a tear from his eye, and said, 'I have never felt more humbled. Truly it is the greatest wish of any musician to have such an appreciative audience. And I would dearly love to play it for you again, but, sadly, I must away to Tel Aviv, where I am due to give another concert this evening.'

At this point a voice from the crowd was heard: 'You must stay here and play it again until you get it right.'

The refined classical musician turns out to be just another shlemiel who, not unlike Kafka's Abraham, imagines applause where there's only derision – only now the mockers are his fellow Jews. (It's why Israelis, despite their rep for bad manners, will never engage in sexual intercourse on the street for fear that a passer-by may stop to point out they're doing it wrong.)

Clearly, then, Israelis are no longer quite the same as those meek and terrified back-of-the-queue Jews we find in jokes about Soviet Russia ...

A journalist asks a Pole, a Russian, an American and an Israeli the same question.

He asks the Pole, 'Excuse me, sir, what is your opinion on the meat shortage?'

The Pole replies, 'What is meat?'

He asks the Russian, 'Excuse me, sir, what is your opinion on the meat shortage?'

The Russian replies, 'What is an opinion?'

He asks the American, 'Excuse me, sir, what is your opinion on the meat shortage?'

The American replies, 'What is a shortage?'

He then asks the Israeli, 'Excuse me, sir, what is your opinion on the meat shortage?'

And the Israeli replies, 'What is "excuse me"?'

But still, there are some things you can't leave behind, and in Israel the Jewish propensity for a gallows sense of humour has not only been sustained, it's if anything intensified:

Anat in Jerusalem hears on the news about a bombing in a popular cafe near the home of relatives in Tel Aviv. She calls in a panic and reaches her cousin, who assures her that the family's OK.

'And Yael?' Anat asks after the teenager who frequents that cafe.

'Oh, Yael,' says her mother reassuringly, 'Yael's fine. She's in Auschwitz.'

... Auschwitz being the fail-safe destination of Israeli school trips.

And the furrowed brow of the optimist hasn't gone away in Israel either:

> Things are going badly for Israel. The occupation, social unrest, the extreme right attacking the extreme left, the economy in a tailspin, inflation getting higher and immigrants flooding in from all over. Problems, problems, problems, but what to do? So the Knesset holds a special session to come up with a solution. After several hours of talk without progress, one member stands up and says, 'Quiet, everyone, I've got it, the solution to all our problems.'

> 'What?'

> 'We'll declare war on the United States.'

> Everyone is shouting at once: 'You're nuts! That's crazy!'

> 'Hear me out!' says the minister. 'We declare war. We lose. The United States does what she always does when she defeats a country. She rebuilds everything – our highways, airports, shipping ports, schools,

hospitals, factories – and loans us money, and sends us food aid. Our problems would be over.'

'Sure,' says another member, '*if* we lose.'

So the punchlines haven't died, they've merely relocated:

Four Israelis have arranged to meet in a cafe. For a long time, nobody says anything. Then, one man groans, 'Oy.'

'Oy vey,' says a second man.

'Nu,' says the third.

At this, the fourth man gets up from his chair and says, 'If you guys don't stop talking politics, I'm leaving!'

Thus, even in 'Zion' Jews are still kvetching, and still sitting in the dark telling each other the lightbulb-less jokes that remain the most bearable form available for transmitting a traumatic history. Though it's a traumatic transmission that, sadly, doesn't stop there. For just as Diaspora Jews have passed their gallows sense of humour on to Jewish Israelis, Jewish Israelis appear to have passed it on to … Palestinian Israelis.

No one conveys the tragic absurdity of that situation better than the very funny Palestinian-Israeli writer Sayed Kashua, whose novels remind one of Kafka and whose Israeli sitcom, *Arab Labour*, is partly inspired by *Seinfeld*. 'I use a lot of humour,' Kashua remarks, 'and I follow the saying that if you want to tell people the truth, you better make them laugh first, otherwise they will shoot you.' Tragically, he isn't joking. What he *is* doing is knowingly focusing attention on the way in which Palestinians have been inveigled into not only the traumatic aspects of Jewish history, but the mordant wit required to survive it. Thus the uncannily familiar tenor of Kashua's quintessentially outsider comic sensibility turns 'getting' his jokes into an implicit mode of acceptance of the very form of historical recognition that has so far, for Palestinians, been politically denied.

That said, the primary thing Jewish humour seems to have given Kashua is someone to blame for his people's sufferings:

> I couldn't lie any more to my kids, telling them that they are equal citizens in the state of Israel. They cannot be equal because in order to fit in and to be

accepted and to be a citizen in Israel, you need a Jewish mother. So basically what I'm trying to tell my kids is just, it's their mother's fault and it's not my fault.*

A line that's both funny and, potentially, hopeful, if we recall Freud's remark that 'laughing at the same jokes is evidence of far-reaching psychic conformity.' For if two people or peoples can share a laugh, then mightn't it be possible for them to share other things as well?**

---

* From an interview with American NPR in 2016.
** That's the dream, but current reality does not reflect it. Thus in 2014 Kashua lost faith that he could change attitudes in Israel and so uprooted his family to the US – a despairing move reflected in his increasingly sober weekly columns for the Israeli newspaper *Haaretz*. 'To have humour,' he explained, 'you have to have hope.' And here we might again consider David Grossman's rendering of an Israeli comedian whose stand-up act is one of such unmitigated desperation that the Jewish joke, while still being pressed into the service of defence and attack, seems, in this novel, to have finally run out of gas. In an admiring review of the book in the *NYRB*, literary critic Stephen Greenblatt describes it as 'one of the least funny novels I have ever read'.

HOW DO YOU TELL THE DIFFERENCE BETWEEN LIFE AND DEATH?

'They tried to kill us, we survived, let's eat' is the mantra of a people whose history has required them to take crises in their stride. But even then, someone still needs to prepare the food:

> The dutiful Jewish son is sitting at his father's bedside. His father is near death.
>
> Father: 'Son.'
>
> Son: 'Yes, Dad.'
>
> Father (weakly): 'Son. That smell. Is your mother making my favourite cheesecake?'

Son: 'Yes, Dad.'

Father (even weaker): 'Ah, if I could just have one more piece of your mum's cheesecake. Would you get me a piece?'

Son: 'OK, Dad.'

(Son leaves and walks towards the kitchen. After a while the son returns and sits down next to his father again.)

Father: 'Is that you, son?'

Son: 'Yes, Dad.'

Father: 'Did you bring the cheesecake?'

Son: 'No, Dad.'

Father: 'Why? It's my dying wish!'

Son: 'Mum says the cake is for after the funeral.'

And someone still needs to pay for it:

Moshe was on his deathbed and raised his head gently. 'Mendel, are you there?'

'Yes, Moshe, I am here.'

A moment later Moshe said, 'Izzi, are you there?'

His son, Izzi, assured him he was by his side.

'Jessica,' said the ailing Moshe, 'are you there?'

'I'm here, Poppa,' said Jessica, taking his hand.

Moshe raised himself on his elbow. 'Then who the hell is minding the shop?'

Practicality rather than loftiness is the gutsy ghetto answer to life's ultimate situations:

A Jewish grandmother is watching her grandchild playing on the beach when a huge wave comes and takes him out to sea. She pleads, 'Please, God, save my only grandson. I beg of you, bring him back.'

A big wave comes and washes the boy back on to the beach, good as new.

She looks up to heaven and says, 'He had a hat!'

It's about keeping your eye on the ball:

An elderly Jewish man is sideswiped by a bicycle as he is trying to cross the street. After a long five or ten minutes, the ambulance comes and the paramedics put him on a stretcher and lift him into the ambulance, bumping him a bit. As they speed off to the hospital, one of the paramedics puts his hand on the old man's shoulder and asks, 'Are you comfortable?'

The old man shrugs: 'I make a living.'

Without losing your critical powers:

An old Jew gets run over by a car and lies down on the ground, bleeding. A priest happens to pass by and rushes over. As he sees the condition of the man, he says, 'Do you believe in the Father, the Son and the Holy Spirit?'

Says the Jew: 'I'm dying and he's asking me riddles?'

(He's still got it.)

If the suggestion in that joke is that Judaism and

Christianity draw a subtly different line between life and death, we can find a similar idea in an anecdote told by the author of the new constitution of post-apartheid South Africa, Justice Albie Sachs. During his time as an anti-apartheid campaigner, Sachs was the victim of a bomb that had been planted to kill him. When, after awaking in hospital, he realised he'd survived the blast, he was reminded of a Jewish joke:

> Hymie Cohen falls off a bike and as he gets up he makes the four motions of crossing himself and someone says, 'Hymie, I didn't know you were Catholic,' and he says, 'What do you mean, Catholic? Spectacles, testicles, wallet and watch.'

'The first thing Comrade Albie did,' the ANC declared afterwards, 'was reach for his balls!'"

And it's this unswervingly unspiritual response to catastrophe ('still got my testicles, now where's my hat?') that also gave Sachs hope for the future of his country: 'This is how we'll get our new South Africa, the Jewish joke, appealing to the African sense of storytelling.'

So for Jews, you could say, life is where it's at, death

---

* Extracted from a talk given by Justice Albie Sachs in the University of Toronto, 2010.

not so much …

Cohen is on his deathbed and tells his kids to call a priest.

'But, but, but, Dad …'

'Call the priest,' I said.

Wanting to honour his wishes, they call the priest. Cohen insists on converting. Then he gets better. Months go by, a year. He is back on form, going to synagogue, keeping kosher, observing the festivals. They muster the courage and ask him, 'That time on your deathbed, Dad, the conversion – what was that all about?'

'I just figured,' says Cohen, 'better one of them than one of us.'

HOW DO YOU TELL THE DIFFERENCE BETWEEN THE TRINITY AND THE ALMIGHTY?

If Christianity has had an ambivalent relationship to Judaism as both the generator and betrayer of its own creed, Judaism has been no less ambivalent about Christianity:

Three proofs that Jesus was Jewish:

1. He went into his father's business.

2. He lived at home until the age of thirty-three.

3. He was sure his mother was a virgin, and his mother was convinced he was God.

Rendering it a source of pride on the one hand:

> A rabbi once asked his old friend, a priest, 'Could you ever be promoted within your Church?'
>
> The priest says, thoughtfully, 'Well, I could become a bishop.'
>
> The rabbi persists, 'And after that?'
>
> With a pause for consideration, the priest replies, 'Maybe I could be a cardinal, even.'
>
> 'And then?'
>
> After thinking for some time, the priest responds, 'Some day I may even rise to be the Pope.'
>
> But the rabbi is still not satisfied. 'And *then*?'
>
> With an air of incredulity, the priest cries, 'What more could I become? God Himself?'
>
> The rabbi says quietly, 'One of *our* boys made it.'

And a source of perplexity on the other:

A Jewish father was troubled by the way his son had turned out, and went to see his rabbi about it.

'I brought him up in the faith, gave him a very expensive bar mitzvah. Cost me a fortune to educate him. Then he tells me last week he has decided to become a Christian! Rabbi, where did I go wrong?'

'Funny you should come to me,' said the rabbi. 'Like you, I too brought my boy up in the faith, put him through university. Cost me a fortune, then one day he too tells me he has decided to become a Christian.'

'What did you do?' asked the father.

'I turned to God for the answer,' replied the rabbi.

'And what did he say?' pressed the father.

'God said, 'Funny you should come to *me* ...''

Although it's always nice when the two sides can come together:

About a century or two ago, the Pope decided that all the Jews had to leave Rome. Naturally there was a big uproar from the Jewish community. So the Pope made a deal. He would have a religious debate with a member of the Jewish community. If the Jew won, the Jews could stay. If the Pope won, the Jews would leave.

The Jews realised that they had no choice. They looked around for a champion who could defend their faith, but no one wanted to volunteer. It was too risky.

So they finally picked an old man named Moishe, who spent his life sweeping up after people, to represent them. Being old and poor, he had less to lose, so he agreed. He asked only for one addition to the debate. Not being used to saying very much as he cleaned up around the settlement, he asked that neither side be allowed to talk. The Pope agreed.

The day of the great debate came. Moishe and the Pope sat opposite each other for a full minute before the Pope raised his hand and showed three fingers. Moishe looked back at him and raised one finger. The Pope waved his fingers in a circle around his head. Moishe pointed to the ground where he sat. The Pope pulled out a wafer and a glass of wine. Moishe pulled out an apple. The Pope stood up and said, 'I give up. This man is too good. The Jews can stay.'

An hour later, the cardinals were all around the Pope asking him what had happened. The Pope said, 'First I held up three fingers to represent the Trinity. He responded by holding up one finger to remind me that there was still one God common to both our religions. Then I waved my finger around me to show him that God was all around us. He responded by pointing to the ground, showing that God was also right here with us. I pulled out the wine and the wafer to show that God absolves us from our sins. He pulled out an apple to remind me of original sin. He had an answer for everything. 'What could I do?'

Meanwhile, the Jewish community had crowded around Moishe, amazed that this old, almost feeble-minded man had done what all their scholars had insisted was impossible. 'What happened?' they asked.

'Well,' said Moishe, 'first he said to me that the Jews had three days to get out of here. I told him that not one of us was leaving. Then he told me that this whole city would be cleared of Jews. I let him know that we were staying right here.'

'And then?' asked a woman.

Moishe shrugged. 'We broke for lunch.'

Not that one should ever get blindsided by religion:

A priest, an imam and a rabbi are waiting one morning for a particularly slow group of golfers.

The rabbi fumes, 'What's with those guys? We must have been waiting for fifteen minutes!'

The imam chimes in, 'I've never seen such inept golf!'

The priest spies the green-keeper and calls him over. 'Hello, George. Do you have any idea what's wrong with that group ahead of us? They're rather slow, aren't they?'

The green-keeper replies, 'Oh, yes. That's a group of blind firemen. They lost their sight saving our club-house from a fire last year, so we always let them play whenever they like for free.'

The group fall silent for a moment.

The priest says, 'That's so sad. I will say a special prayer for them tonight.'

The imam says, 'Good idea. I'm going to collect charity for them.'

The rabbi says, 'They couldn't play at night?'

Though this is a joke in which Judaism retains its reputation as a worldly religion with an emphasis on practical (win-win) solutions, Jewish charity doesn't look too worthy when contrasted with the other religions out there on the golf course. Were you to hear this joke told by a non-Jew, therefore, you might find yourself worrying about the teller's motive – inviting the question: *is* it ever possible for someone who isn't Jewish to tell that kind of joke with a clear conscience ... *just* for a laugh?

And funnily enough, the blind golfers joke *is* related in a recent American novel, *To Rise Again at a Decent Hour* (2014), by the non-Jewish writer Joshua Ferris. The joke is told by the protagonist, a dentist who, like the dentist in *Seinfeld*, is hoping to convert to a version of what he understands to be Judaism primarily by means of telling Jewish jokes. And as in *Seinfeld* also, the dentist in the novel tells the joke poorly, with comically bad timing. He's accused of this by his unsmiling Jewish girlfriend:

> 'Why,' I said, 'is it anti-Semitic? It's not anti-Semitic, is it?'

> I was always paranoid that I might be saying something anti-Semitic.

Always paranoid? *That* sounds (Jewishly) familiar.

HOW DO YOU TELL THE DIFFERENCE BETWEEN MAN AND GOD?

While Jews don't accept the Christian belief that a man can also be a divinity, they're generally pretty good at spotting the human side of the godly:

Moshe and Abe were partners in a very successful clothing factory. It had been in operation for many years and there wasn't much they didn't know about the shmatta business [rag trade]. One day, Moshe decided to take a trip to Rome.

As Abe had many Catholic friends, he surprised Moshe by getting him an audience with none other than the Pope.

On Moshe's first day back at work after his Rome trip, Abe asked him, 'So, Moshe! What kind of a man is the Pope?'

'Hmm,' said Moshe, 'I would say he's a 44 regular.'

And when it comes to the Almighty, Jews tend to take things pretty personally too. As Sholom Aleichem's character Tevye complains to God:

'*You help complete strangers – why* not me?'

But then, when you know someone *that* long and still they turn a cold shoulder, it's hard to keep up the pretence that it *isn't* personal:

A journalist heard about a very old Jewish man who had been going to the Western Wall to pray twice a day, every day, for a long, long time, so she went to check it out. She went to the Western Wall and there he was, walking slowly up to the holy site. She watched him pray and after about forty-five minutes, when he turned to leave, using a cane and moving very slowly, she approached him for an interview.

'Pardon me, sir. What's your name?

'Morris Feinberg,' he replied.

'Sir, how long have you been coming to the Western Wall and praying?'

'For about sixty years.'

'Sixty years! That's amazing! What do you pray for?'

'I pray for peace between the Christians, Jews and the Muslims. I pray for all the wars and all the hatred to stop. I pray for all our children to grow up safely as responsible adults, and to love their fellow man.'

'How do you feel after doing this for sixty years?'

'Like I'm talking to a bloody wall.'

Jews have long since realised that God can be something of a let-down:

Moses is walking in the hills. He slips. Finding himself hanging between heaven and earth, he calls out: 'Is there anyone there?'

A voice responds from above: 'Yes, I'm here. It's God. Don't worry, I'll save you.'

Pause.

Moses: 'Is there anyone else there?'

Which doesn't mean God is a bad guy. Rather, as Woody Allen has it, 'You know, if it turns out that there *is* a *God*, I don't think that *He's* evil. I think that the worst *you can say* about Him is that, basically, *He's an underachiever*'*:

A man brings some very fine material to a tailor and asks him to make a pair of trousers. When he comes back a week later, the trousers are not ready. Two weeks later, they are still not ready. Finally, after six weeks, the trousers are ready. The man tries them on. They fit perfectly. Nonetheless, when it comes time to pay, he can't resist a jibe at the tailor.

'You know,' he says, 'it took God only six days to make the world. And it took you six weeks to make just one pair of trousers.'

* From *Love and Death* (1975).

'Ah,' the tailor says. 'But look at this pair of trousers, and look at the world...'

So the world was a bit of a rushed job. And if that explains the state of the world, then it also explains why man, as the product of just one day's work, isn't exactly an overachiever either:

Moishe is driving in Jerusalem. He's late for a meeting and he's looking and failing to find a parking place. In desperation, he turns towards heaven and says, 'Lord, if you find me a parking place, I promise that I'll eat only kosher, respect Shabbos and all the holidays.' Miraculously, a place opens up just in front of him. He turns his face up to heaven and says, 'Never mind, I just found one!'

Because when you get a shlemiel people, you're bound to get a shlimazel God:

There is this very pious Jew named Goldberg who always dreamed of winning the lottery. Every Sabbath, he'd go to synagogue and pray, 'God, I have been such a pious Jew all my life. What would be so bad if I won the lottery?'

But the lottery would come and Goldberg wouldn't win. Week after week, Goldberg would pray to win the lottery, but the lottery would come and Goldberg wouldn't win.

Finally, one Sabbath, Goldberg wails to the heavens and says, 'God, I have been so pious for so long, what do I have to do to win the lottery?'

And the heavens parted and the voice of God came down: 'Goldberg, meet me halfway. At least buy a ticket.'

Though never say the people don't at least *try*:

God: And remember, Moses, in the laws of keeping kosher, never cook a calf in its mother's milk. It is cruel.

Moses: Ohhhhhh! So you are saying we should never eat milk and meat together.

God: No, what I'm saying is, never cook a calf in its mother's milk.

Moses: Oh, Lord, forgive my ignorance! What you are really saying is we should wait six hours after eating meat to eat milk so the two are not in our stomachs.

God: No, Moses, what I'm saying is, don't cook a calf in its mother's milk!

Moses: Oh, Lord! Please don't strike me down for my stupidity! What you mean is we should have a separate set of dishes for milk and a separate set for meat and if we make a mistake we have to bury that dish outside ...

God: Ach, do whatever you want ...

Thus, just because the Jewish joke tends to be more logistical than spiritual, doesn't mean it's not serious – *even* about God. We might see it instead as an extension of the Jewish covenantal tradition that sees man in a partnership with God. Albeit a partnership that gives him, just as it gives God, the right to kvetch.

HOW DO YOU TELL THE DIFFERENCE BETWEEN A GOOD JOKE AND A BAD JOKE?

Jews get a lot of laughs out of God. But how godly is the joke?

In the Jewish joke, sometimes godliness is a source of wisdom:

A Hasid comes to see his rabbi.

'Rabbi, I have had a dream in which I am the leader of three hundred Hasidim.'

The rabbi replies: 'Come back when three hundred Hasidim have had a dream that you are their leader.'

Yet at other times it's a mockery of wisdom:

> A man was boasting about his rabbi: 'My rabbi is so
> modest about his piety. If he eats, it is only to hide
> from others the fact that he is fasting.'

Believers in comedy will often invoke the subversive power of joking to keep us honest by ridiculing the pretensions of the powerful. Yet we know, of course, that the joke is just as often a tool *of* the powerful to make laughing stocks of the weak. And that, as positions and perspectives constantly slip, slide and change, the identity of who is powerful and who weak is seldom set in stone. Thus, while we might be perfectly within our rights to send someone up one day, we may be abusing an unfair advantage if we do so the next. There are few utterances more flush with unchecked privilege, after all, than the sneering sound of someone insisting, in the face of another's hurt, that they really ought to be able to 'take a joke'.

It's the job of the comedian, therefore, to gauge what is and isn't 'fair game', which is another way of saying that a comic requires a sense of that other slippery concept: justice.* And they require it not least

---

* Interpreting a verse from Ecclesiastes, 'And God will seek the pursued', the
  rabbis of the Talmud suggest that God is always shifting positions to take the

because by being as clear-eyed and non-prejudicial as possible about the times in which they're living, comedians can hone their sense of timing to make their acts that bit funnier:

> Every incredible achievement in human history was done with slaves. Every single thing where you go, 'How did they build those pyramids?' They just threw human death and suffering at them until they were finished . . . Even today, how do we have this amazing micro-technology? Because the factory where they make them, they jump off the fucking roof because it's a nightmare in there. You really have a choice: you can have candles and horses and be a little kinder to each other, or let someone far away suffer immeasurably so you can leave a mean comment on YouTube. *Louis C.K.*[*]

Of course, the (good) comedian doesn't imagine he's any better than the time he's telling. (The fact, for example, that Louis C.K. has tended to make self-admonishments at his own moral failings a constant theme of his comedy was brutally revealed to be no laughing matter.[**]) But what the comedian possibly

side of the pursued over that of the pursuer, regardless of each figure's moral character or social identity.

[*] From his HBO stand-up special *Oh My God* (2013).

[**] On Nov 10 2017, in a letter in the NYT responding to allegations by a number

does get better than most is that no one can claim to be entirely innocent when they're laughing:

A Nazi sees a Jew walking towards him.

As the Jew passes by, the Nazi says 'Swine!'

The Jew tips his hat and says, 'Cohen.'

Or:

An old Jew was refused service in a restaurant.

'We don't serve Jews here,' said the waiter.

'Don't let that bother you,' replied the old man. 'I don't eat Jews.'

Neither of these jokes strikes me as laugh-out-loud funny. But if we see the punchline as mocking by resembling the original attempt at a put-down, we can see the joke as a means of showing how a lousy sense of humour can always get its comeuppance.

What typifies a lousy sense of humour? I'd say it's

of female comics that he had sexually harassed them, C.K. confessed that 'these stories are true.'

a failure to understand the material it's working with.
And by material I mean *words*, as slippery as any
banana skin:

> I had dinner with my father last night, and I made
> a classic Freudian slip. I meant to say, 'Please pass
> the salt,' but it came out, 'You putz, you ruined my
> childhood!' *Jonathan Katz*

Words have a funny habit of turning their sense around
to make the teller of the joke the butt of the joke. It's
the reason why most jokes in circulation appear un-
authored, as if they'd erupted autonomously out of
our everyday language, laying waste to common sense.
Indeed, it's precisely because jokes appear disparaging
of anything so proprietorial as authorship or beard-
stroking authority that they're broadly untroubled by
issues of copyright (hence why I can raid other people's
joke-book collections for favourite examples in my
own). So are our jokes then evidence that our words
may be laughing *at* us? In which case, language would
be just like the God who laughs when you tell Him your
plans – the God who, as Heinrich Heine intimated, is
nothing if not an ironist.*

---

* The German romantic poet Heinrich Heine (1797–1856), who was born into a
  Jewish family but later converted to Lutheranism (which didn't prevent his be-

Perhaps the difference between a bad and a good joke, then, is not unlike the difference between sarcasm and irony. Sarcasm pokes fun without any notion that there may be something misunderstood or unrecognised about the object of its derision (I'm so *obviously* right about this).[*] Irony, though, gestures towards the unknown and unknowable, getting laughs precisely at the point where other, more direct, forms of representation have reached their limits. Hence if sarcasm suggests a know-it-all attitude, irony, *pace* Socrates,[**] finds the funniness where it *knows it knows nothing*:

> Moskowitz and Finkelstein were in a cafeteria, drinking tea. Moskowitz studied his cup and said with a sigh, 'Ah, my friend, life is like a cup of tea.'

> Finkelstein considered that for a moment and then said, 'But why is life like a cup of tea?'

> Moskowitz replied, 'How should I know? Am I a philosopher?'

coming the target of anti-Semitic attacks and subsequently Nazi demonisation), attested to 'God's irony' and 'the irony of the great poet of the world stage up there'.

[*] Though I align it for the sake of argument with nominally 'bad' humour here, I don't deny that sarcasm is often merited, nor that it can be extremely funny.

[**] The Greek philosopher identified by Kierkegaard as the world's greatest ironist.

HOW DO YOU TELL THE DIFFERENCE BETWEEN COMEDY AND THEOLOGY?

One common rendering of today's typically religious person is someone with so many sacred cows that they're constantly taking offence. A comedian, on the other hand, in the popular imagination, is someone for whom nothing is sacred – it's someone who gives offence rather than taking it. And yet if there's one thing that *can* be guaranteed to offend comedians, it's sacred cows. Be they religious pieties, social snobberies or political correctnesses, sacred cows are like red flags to the comedian's bull. In fact, they attack them with such missionary zeal, it's almost as if some sacred cow of their own was driving their iconoclasm. So what, we might ask, is the comedian's sacred cow?

Back in the shtetl, Moishe was in his bed, dying. They brought him fresh milk from the cow to help him feel less parched, but he was too weak to get out any words. Maybe, his daughter thought, some spirits could help revive him. She put a little whisky in with the milk and gave it to him. Moishe shot bolt upright in bed and said his immortal last words: 'Don't sell the cow!'

Okay, okay, so that's not the comedian's sacred cow ...

A rabbinical student is about to set off on his first job in a far-flung community away from everyone he knows. He asks his own rabbi, a famous scholar of the Talmud, for some final words of wisdom before he leaves.

'Life is a fountain,' his teacher tells him. The young rabbi is moved by the profundity of those words as he embarks on a hugely successful career.

Many years later, hearing his teacher is dying, he visits him one last time. 'Rabbi,' he says, 'I have one question for you. For so many years now, whenever I've been sad or confused, I've told myself that "life is a fountain" – your words of precious wisdom – and that thought has always helped me get through even the worst of times, and yet truth be told I have never really understood what that adage means. Please can you tell me: *why* is life a fountain?'

'All right,' says his rabbi wearily, 'so life *isn't* a fountain.'

Sometimes, that is, a joke is just a joke. And not only that: the acceptance of chance, accident and contingency ought to even be considered a condition of possibility of the joke. For while theologians are tempted to see everything as part of a divine plan, comics find their freedom in the right to be *unserious* – and in the distinctly profane enjoyment to be had in the spectacle of a serious man, a man in a business suit, who is walking determinedly to work when, for no apparent reason, he slips and finds himself flat out on the ground.

In admitting that, however, can we ever be *entirely* sure when a slip is just a slip, a joke just a joke, a kiss just a kiss, or even a cigar just a cigar? It was Søren Kierkegaard, after all, one of the greatest modern theologians, who, when faced with the hapless man in a business suit, could not but detect the divine comedy at work: '[When] a tile from the roof falls down and strikes him dead, then I laugh heartily.'* And whether or not you're tempted to join him in that confounding laughter, you can hardly fail to notice the irony or self-contradiction of an essay strung together by jokes attempting to make a case for the joke as that which radically refuses the kind of meaning or determination that it might expect to receive in an essayistic interpretation.

Thus, while there's some truth to the idea that a comedian is someone prepared to transgress laws, rules and reasons – or do *anything* for a laugh – there are nonetheless limits to the liberties any such comedian will likely take. Most comedians, for example, *do* have lines they won't cross or things they feel they can't say without doing damage to the funny. As Jerry Seinfeld tells the priest, he's offended by his dentist's conversion, not as a Jewish person but as a *comedian*. Because not everyone gets to tell the same jokes as well as each other. His dentist, Jerry thinks, is acquiring 'joke-telling immunity' by underhand means – he's converting to Judaism not as a creed, but as a sense of humour. And you can't convert to a sense of humour, can you? I mean, much as he'd love to, Jerry doesn't get to tell all of Richard Pryor's jokes.

* *Either/Or, Part 1* (1843).

You can't *convert* to blackness, no more than you can to whiteness:

> People are always introducing me as 'Sarah Silverman, Jewish comedienne'. I *hate* that! I wish people would see me for who I really am – I'm *white*!

Or can you?

HOW DO YOU TELL THE DIFFERENCE BETWEEN JEWISH AND GOYISH?

Here's how Lenny Bruce tells it:

> Dig: I'm Jewish. Count Basie's Jewish. Ray Charles is
> Jewish. Eddie Cantor's goyish. B'nai B'rith is goyish;
> Hadassah, Jewish. If you live in New York or any
> other big city, you are Jewish. It doesn't matter even
> if you're Catholic; if you live in New York, you're
> Jewish. If you live in Butte, Montana, you're going to
> be goyish even if you're Jewish.
>
> Kool-Aid is goyish. Evaporated milk is goyish, even
> if the Jews invented it. Chocolate is Jewish and fudge
> is goyish. Fruit salad is Jewish. Lime jello is goyish.
> Lime soda is very goyish.

All Drake's Cakes are goyish. Pumpernickel is Jewish and, as you know, white bread is very goyish. Instant potatoes, goyish. Black cherry soda's very Jewish, macaroons are very Jewish.

Negroes are all Jews. Italians are all Jews. Irishmen who have rejected their religion are Jews. Mouths are very Jewish. And bosoms. Baton-twirling is very goyish.

Underwear is definitely goyish. Balls are goyish. Titties are Jewish.

Celebrate is a goyish word. *Observe* is a Jewish word. Mr and Mrs Walsh are celebrating Christmas with Major Thomas Moreland, USAF (ret.), while Mr and Mrs Bromberg observed Hanukkah with Goldie and Arthur Schindler from Kiamesha, New York.

Bruce, one suspects, almost *could* have got away with telling Richard Pryor's jokes.* For what he's suggesting in this sketch is a whole new way of telling the difference. Neither Jewish nor goyish are

---

* And vice versa. Richard Pryor once claimed to owe his career to Lenny Bruce: 'I played his record over and over, every night. It was him who said comedy wasn't about telling jokes – it was about telling the truth.'

absolute categories – everyone is who they are-*ish* –
hence you can count yourself among the Jew-*ish* set
of differences if you like Bruce's shtick and you laugh
along with his jokes.

And it's on the same basis, presumably, that you can
convert to blackness. Or to whiteness. Or to a sense
of humour. In fact, why not go further still? Maybe
converting to a sense of humour *is* the most authentic
means of conversion. Because isn't it the moment
when someone *gets* our jokes or finds the same things
funny as we do that we *do*, implicitly, recognise them
as one of our own kind? (Note that, before it found
its way into the annals of Jewish joking, the whisky-
mixing cow started out on an Irish dairy farm in a joke
about a dying Mother Superior surrounded by nuns
who were already showing their talent for serving
more than one order of high spirits.)

And Bruce's sense of his own Jew-*ish* kind was
the nervous kind, the vulnerable kind, the willing
to show you're flawed, human and mortal kind. So
he'd have likely agreed with Jerry's dentist about
the sustaining power of humour. If, that is, Bruce
could spot his own peeps everywhere, it's because he
recognised something critical about the funny – how
it's always got a hidden history of suffering buried
somewhere inside it:

A black man was reading a Yiddish newspaper on the New York subway.

Someone stops and asks, 'Are you Jewish?'

'Oy gevalt,' he replies, 'that's the *last* thing I need.'

Since a sense of humour surely *is* what he needs, however, he's a man who makes perfect sense in the Jewish joke.

'Every black man,' the narrator of Paul Beatty's extremely funny novel *The Sellout* (2015) confesses, secretly thinks he can 'tell jokes' better than anyone else in the world. And we get from the novel why that is: because of the suffering, pain, powerlessness and diverted aggression and anger that goes into it. It's this, in fact, that comes into sharp focus at the conclusion of the novel, which winds up at a stand-up gig in which a black comedian admonishes the white couple in the front row for laughing at his jokes. In a reverse heckle that's completely serious, although the couple at first assume he must be joking, he tells them to 'get the fuck out!' because 'This is our thing!' The problem, this comedian implies, with the white people laughing along with his act, is that they don't really *get* what they're laughing at. And the same, naturally, may be true for the white people laughing along with Beatty's novel. Although the narrator's subsequent question – 'So what exactly is *our thing*?' – sounds a little more dubious than is the comedian about the rules of belonging. Which, arguably, was also Bruce's point: that just as joking is slippery, so must its recipients be. For while it's true that no joke can be for everyone – and the joke will always depend on someone being 'in' on it, and someone left out – stand-up, being very much a 'live' act, can have no guarantees in advance as to who, if anyone, will find it funny.

Not, it's important to add, that comedy is the *only* creative outlet for historical suffering:

> We've come from the same history – two thousand years of persecution – we've just expressed our sufferings differently. Blacks developed the blues. Jews complained – we just never thought of putting it to music. *Jon Stewart*

HOW DO YOU TELL THE DIFFERENCE BETWEEN SPORTING AND JOKING?

So let's return to the analogy we've spoken of between religious persons and comedians, which is starting now to make some sense – for if the religious person appears as one kind of extremist, the comedian appears as another. It was Lenny Bruce who led the way here by turning stand-up into something of an extreme sport. And thank heavens for that, because Jews, on the whole, aren't too good at sports:

> Yeshiva University decided to field a crew in the rowing race. Unfortunately, they lost race after race. They practised for hours every day, but never managed to come in any better than dead last.

The chief rabbi finally decided to send Yankel to spy on the Harvard team. So Yankel goes to Cambridge and hid in the bullrushes off the Charles River, from where he carefully watched the Harvard team as they practised.

Yankel finally returned to Yeshiva. 'I have figured out their secret,' he announced. 'They have eight guys rowing and only one guy shouting.'

Extreme talking, you could say, is the *aim* of the Jewish athlete:

The rabbi was an avid golfer and played at every opportunity. He was so addicted to the game that if he didn't play he would get withdrawal symptoms. One Yom Kippur the rabbi thought to himself, 'What's it going to hurt if I go out during the recess and play a few rounds? Nobody will be the wiser, and I'll be back in time for services.'

Sure enough, at the conclusion of the morning service, the rabbi snuck out of the synagogue and headed straight for the golf course. Looking down upon the scene were Moses and God.

Moses said, 'Look how terrible – a Jew on Yom Kippur. And a rabbi besides!'

God replied, 'Watch. I'm going to teach him a lesson.'

Out on the course, the rabbi stepped up to the first tee. When he hit the ball, it careened off a tree, struck a rock, skipped across a pond and landed in the hole for a HOLE IN ONE!

Seeing all this, Moses protested, 'God, this is how you're going to teach him a lesson? He got a hole in one!'

'Sure,' said God, 'but who's he going to tell?'

But if not being able to tell is the cruellest punishment for a Jew who's indulged his guilty pleasure, telling the things you *can't* tell is a guilty pleasure all of its own – as in the joke about the guy who goes to confession and tells the priest that after a lifetime of respectability he suddenly finds himself having an affair with two young married women half his age. When the priest urges him to seek Jesus' forgiveness he replies that he can't do that because he's Jewish. 'Then why on earth are you telling me?' 'I'm telling *everyone*.'

Or you need only consider the taboo-breaking excitement of a Lenny Bruce gig. In his major novel *Underworld* (1997), the American author Don DeLillo captures that atmosphere by imagining a scene in which Bruce is performing a set in California during the Cuban Missile Crisis. The set has just one 'joke', but it's one he tells over and over again to evermore nervous laughter:

'We're all gonna die!'

Hahahahahahahahahahahahahahaha.

Darkness, death, war, the unknown, the unknowable – that's where the nervous laughter comes from. And both the Jewish person and the comedian are familiars here. Both know what it is to perform in front of hostile crowds, always with the aim of trying to get the audience on side. Both have felt the need to constantly adapt their acts and find a quick-fire response for the latest hecklers. And both also recognise the fatal consequences of not being approved of. Jews know this in their (funny) bones. And a bad night for a comedian is one when nobody finds their shtick funny. When that happens, the comedian will tell you, they 'died'.

HOW DO YOU TELL THE DIFFERENCE?

On Passover, Jews ask the question 'Why is this night different from all other nights?' But *is* it so different? Not in one respect, at least: asking why anything is different from anything else *isn't* especially unusual for Jews.

If Jews love anything, it's telling the difference. What's kosher or unkosher? Milky or meaty? Circumcised or uncircumcised? Thirst or diabetes? In yeshivas (religious schools), Jews study the Talmud and the law, always with an eye on how to tell the minutest distinctions between seemingly similar things. Sometimes the difference simply comes down to how you ask the question:

Two yeshiva students, Yankel and Moshe, discuss whether it is permitted to smoke while learning Torah. They disagree. Yankel says, 'I will go and ask the rabbi.'

Yankel: 'Rabbi, is it permitted to smoke while learning Torah?'

Rabbi states in a severe tone: 'No!'

Moshe: 'Rabbi, let me ask you another question. May we learn Torah while we smoke?'

Rabbi, benign: 'Yes, of course!'

But at other times differences are maintained far more strictly:

A modern, orthodox Jewish couple, preparing for a religious wedding, meet with their rabbi. The rabbi asks if they have any last questions before they leave.

The man asks, 'Rabbi, we realise it's tradition for men to dance with men, and women to dance with women, at the reception. But we'd like your permission to dance together.'

'Absolutely not,' says the rabbi. 'It's immodest. Men and women always dance separately.'

'So after the ceremony I can't even dance with my own wife?'

'No,' answered the rabbi. 'It's forbidden.'

'Well, OK,' says the man, 'what about sex? Can we finally have sex?'

'Of course!' replies the rabbi. 'Sex is a mitzvah within marriage.'

'What about different positions?' asks the man.

'No problem,' says the rabbi. 'It's a mitzvah!'

'Woman on top?' the man asks.

'Sure,' says the rabbi. 'Go for it!'

'Doggy style?'

'Sure! Another mitzvah!'

'On the kitchen table?'

'Yes, yes! A mitzvah!'

'Can we do it standing up?'

'No,' says the rabbi.

'Why not?' asks the man.

'It could lead to dancing!'

This obsession with telling the difference forms a big part of Alexander Portnoy's complaint about a family endlessly invested in keeping up with the Cohens and telling their difference from the Joneses – not to mention their effort to keep up with the Joneses and tell their difference from the Cohens. And it was precisely this kind of point-scoring that Freud also identified and called 'the narcissism of small differences' (show-off). Lenny Bruce, meanwhile, tells the difference between Jewish and goyish differently – but still, the point is he *tells* it.

However if 'How do you tell the difference?'

is the Jewish question par excellence, it's also, as we've seen, the standard question of any number of classical jokes. So isn't *that* telling? The joke we told earlier, for example, about how to tell the difference between a Jew and an anti-Semite ...

> The anti-Semite thinks the Jews are a despicable race, but Cohen? He's not too bad actually. Kushner? A stand-up guy. The Jew, on the other hand, believes his people are a light unto the nations, but Cohen? What a shmuck! Kushner? Don't get me started!

... is a joke that gains its humour from the fact that this difference turns out to be a surprisingly subtle one. Yet it's precisely the seeming smallness of the difference that shows us why the joke is Jewish rather than anti-Semitic. For while the anti-Semite may imagine that categories and people are so completely opposed that they have nothing whatsoever to do with each other, the Jewish joke understands that every self is fractured and run through with otherness. Everyone is split by something unassimilable or strange: the sense of difference within that puts each of us in an eternal double act with all others, including those others posing as ourselves. Consider, for instance, the words of Groucho Marx's Captain

Spaulding in the film *Animal Crackers* (1930):

> Spaulding: Say, I used to know a fellow looked exactly
> like you, by the name of ... ah ... Emanuel Ravelli.
> Are you his brother?
>
> Ravelli: I'm Emanuel Ravelli.
>
> Spaulding: You're Emanuel Ravelli?
>
> Ravelli: I'm Emanuel Ravelli.
>
> Spaulding: Well, no wonder you look like him ... But
> I still insist, there is a resemblance.

What Jewish jokes consistently reveal is much the same: there's always some sort of doubleness at play in Jewish identity, just as there is in joking itself, or in language itself. And it's this doubleness that makes even the truth a kind of lie ('You say you're going to Minsk and I happen to know you really *are* going to Minsk, so why are you lying to me?'), which is probably what's so funny about the truth – the reason why it tickles us.

So what, then, *is* the difference between a Jewish person and a comedian? Is it simply a question of distinguishing the funny peculiar from the funny ha ha? Or might it be that those two types of funny are as inseparable from each other as are Laurel and Hardy, Laverne and Shirley,* or any other shlemiel/shlimazel comedy double act? Besides, can we even *tell* if it's the fall guy or the straight guy who we're laughing at? What if the funny ha ha of the shlemiel's various pratfalls is really just a cover story for exposing how funny peculiar the supposedly 'straight guy' is?

Even Emanuel Ravelli is only *passing* as Emanuel Ravelli, after all. And even those things we would most dearly like to believe are unquestionable, universal, and completely unmarked by differences, have a tendency to mislead us:

A non-Jewish maths teacher gets a job in a Jewish primary school.

'Are you concerned at all, since you're not Jewish yourself, about what it might be like teaching Jewish children?' the head teacher asks him.

'Not remotely,' says the teacher. 'I teach mathematics,

---

* Laverne and Shirley were the female co-stars of an American sitcom in the late 1970s to early 1980s, whose theme song opened, 'One, two, three, four, five, six, seven, eight, shlemiel, shlimazel   '

and maths knows neither creed nor colour nor age nor gender – it's a universal language, and that's what makes it beautiful.'

Next day, the teacher teaches his first class. He draws a diagram on the blackboard and asks, 'What's two per cent?'

At which point a small boy in the front row opens out his palms, shrugs his shoulders and admits, 'You're right.'*

There are a great many things one could find to say about a young boy for whom mathematics is just another vernacular – a set of rules more practical than Platonic, a language of compromise, of give and take – but this joke is no more about mathematics than the joke about conversion is about Christianity, or the joke about queuing about communism. Rather, what all these Jewish jokes have in common is the conviction that universal claims, whether made in the name of religion, politics, science or even golf, always leave someone on the outside – someone who sees or hears things differently:

---

* Most jokes are best heard aloud, but this one especially.

At Columbia University [this one's meant to be a true anecdote] the great linguist J. L. Austin once gave a lecture about language in which he explained how many languages employ the double negative to denote a positive – 'he is not unlike his sister', for example. 'But there exists no language in which the equivalent is true,' said Austin. 'There is no language that employs a double positive to make a negative.' At this point the philosopher Sidney Morgenbesser, sitting at the back of the lecture theatre, could be heard audibly scoffing, 'Yeah, yeah.'

Telling the difference, in other words, is a way of telling the truth *about* language – about how language is nothing *but* difference:

Before the war, there was a great international Esperanto convention in Geneva. Esperanto scholars came from all over the world to give papers about, and to praise the idea of, an international language. Every country on earth was represented at the convention, and all the papers were given in Esperanto. After the long meeting was finally concluded, the great scholars wandered amiably along the corridors, and at last they felt free to talk casually among themselves in their international language: 'Nu, vos macht a yid?'

That, for those in the know, is a Yiddish 'how do you do'. Indeed Esperanto, another modern utopian dream of a universal system – in this case the dream of a universal language – was invented by a Polish Jew, L. L. Zamenhof.* So what are we to make of this? That only those who've been forced to *feel* their differences would dream up such hare-brained schemes for overcoming them ...?

Possibly. And yet another Jewish philosopher, Jacques Derrida, doesn't think differences *can* be overcome. In fact, for Derrida, *all* language tells of difference (and even the word *difference* is one he inflects with a subtle semantic difference, spelling it 'différance'). Here, accordingly, is his take on another classic Jewish joke:

There are three people isolated on an island: a German citizen, a French citizen and a Jew, totally alone on this island. They don't know when they will leave the island, and it is boring.

One of them says, 'Well, we should do something. We should do something, the three of us. Why don't we write something on the elephants?' There were a number of elephants on the island. 'Everyone should

* He was also responsible for writing the first published grammar of Yiddish.

write something on the elephants and then we could compare the styles and the national idioms,' and so on and so forth.

So the week after, the French one came, with a short, brilliant, witty essay on the sexual drive, or sexual appetite, of the elephants; very short, bright and brilliant essay, very, very superficial but very brilliant. Three months or three years after that, the German came with a heavy book on the … let's say a very positive scientific book on the comparison between two kinds of species, with a very scientific title, endless title for a very positive scientific book on the elephants and the ecology of the elephants on the island. And the two of them asked the Jew, 'Well, when will you give us your book?'

'Wait, it's a very serious question. I need more time. I need more time.'

And they came again every year asking him for his book. Finally, after ten years, he came back with a book called 'The Elephant and the Jewish Question'.

Faced with the Jewish question, the question of difference itself, you always need to defer the answer

(Derrida's 'différance' is a composite of *difference* and *deferral*). You always need more time – so much time, in fact, that the Jewish question has made something of a shaggy dog story out of Jewish history:

> A young Jewish Frenchman brought his trousers to a tailor to have them altered. But by the next day France was occupied and it was too dangerous for Jews to appear in public. He hid underground. Soon enough he got involved in the Resistance. He eventually found his way to a boat and managed to escape the death camps of Europe. He settled in Israel. Ten years later he returned to France. While dressing, he reached into his jacket pocket and found the tailor's receipt for his trousers. He went to look for the tailor's shop and, amazingly, it was still there. He handed the tailor the receipt and asked, 'Are my trousers here?'
>
> 'Yes, of course,' said the tailor. 'Be ready next Tuesday.'

And yet the fact that the Jewish question, like the Jewish joke, endures, finding itself constantly repeated and recycled, as if no change in time or place or polity could make the blindest bit of difference, is also cause for a very Jewish kind of optimism:

On the eve of the Day of Atonement, when all Jews are asked to seek forgiveness, two Jews who hate one another see each other in shul.

One approaches the other and says, 'I wish for you everything that you wish for me.'

The other replies, '*Already*, you're starting again?'

Never forget the Dropkin fart! For it's a joke to imagine the slate can be so easily wiped clean, just as it's a folly to presume that hostilities can be easily upended or differences simply overcome. And Jewish jokes all pay homage to such a world: a world that's complicated, non-homogeneous and full of irreconcilable differences.* But yeah, yeah, who says repetition *doesn't* make a difference? For though he may well have given up all hope of reconciliation because he finds his rival *un*bearable, each man in the Yom Kippur joke *does* briefly bear with the other man. And isn't it precisely that bearable/unbearable coming together in an intimate space, where one doesn't deny one's contradictions, confusions and

---

* Which is why the mainstreaming of Jewish humour in America especially should not be read as a trend towards universalising the joke, but should rather be understood the other way round: as a sign that more and more people may be feeling themselves outsiders.

differences, the dynamic that's at play in every good joke?

Just as tickling isn't stroking, laughter has something of aggression in it. But given the capacity of the funny to sustain differences, contradictions and uncertainties rather than seeking their obliteration, it's generally a better way of dealing with aggression than the alternatives. Thus, if Jews have, at certain points in their history, developed a particular appreciation for the funny side, it's likely because they've needed to mitigate the terrors of a world in which differences are no longer tolerated.* One need only look at the fate of 'the Jewish question' for example. The questions faced by post-Enlightenment Jews – 'What is the nature of your identity? What unites you as a group? What makes you different?' – would prove so incredibly dangerous because Jews

---

* Of course, there are plenty of Jews who neither joke nor get tickled by jokes. Such humourlessness merits its own historical explanation. It's not my purpose here to suggest one, but I will briefly draw attention to two different types of humourlessness hinted at in David Grossman's unfunny book about a comedian. One of these is fair game for the caustic stand-up: 'Have you ever seen a lefty laugh? ... they just can't see the humour in the situation.' You can poke fun at lefties, in other words, for their sententiousness, for their political correctness and for their implicit bad faith. But the novel also features a less partisan example: a disturbingly child-like looking older member of the audience who is always in earnest and who functions as a kind of conscience for the stand-up who will show no mercy to anyone *except* for this 'tiny woman' whom he dimly recalls from his own childhood as the other troubled kid on the block to become an object of derision and general punch-bag, but who never learned, as he did, to take on that sadism and use it as a tool of survival in a harsh and pitiless world.

were unable to answer them in a manner that could satisfy their interrogators. *What*, their interrogators wanted to know, were they hiding? After all, nothing provokes aggression like the feeling that those one finds funny (peculiar) must be sharing some sort of secret joke with each other (ha ha). And there's little worse than the thought that other people may be secretly or not so secretly laughing *at* us.

So it is that Jewish comedians have tended to cover their own backs with self-deprecation – because they *get* how nervous laughter is. Indeed, if Don DeLillo's Lenny Bruce inspires increasingly nervous laughs by saying 'We're all gonna die!' over and over again, the rabbi turned stand-up comedian Jackie Mason has been able to elicit equally manic laughter from his audiences by saying just one word over and over again:

Jew. Jew. Jew. Jew. Jew.

Clearly there isn't, for Mason, all that much of a difference between a Jew and a joke. Not when it's possible to pare down his act to this one lonely word, saying it over and over until the whole room is in hysterics. Or, rather, all the Jews are laughing, and all the non-Jews are wondering what the hell the Jews are laughing about ('Hmmm, I always *knew* there was something funny about those peculiar people').

But why is the word *Jew* sometimes funny? For if the same 'joke' were told by a non-Jew, wouldn't a very different kind of audience be cracking up at it? The word or the joke would be exactly the same, but wouldn't that comedy now be a kind of hate speech? So who gets to decide that the word *Jew* is or isn't a joke? And how can you tell the difference between this joke when it's told by a Jewish comedian or an anti-Semitic one?

What about when the (partly Jewish, though mostly lapsed Catholic) comedian Louis C.K. tells it for example – a comic who, as we mentioned before, is no stranger to causing offense? 'Jew,' C.K. notes in one of his sets, is 'the only word that is the polite thing to call a group of people and the slur for the same group ... It's the same word, just with a little stank on it, and it becomes a terrible thing to call a person.' So not unlike Mason, and to similarly irrepressible laughter, C.K. has also tried out the good and the bad 'Jew' on audiences:

Jew. *Jew*. Jew. *Jew*. Jew.

Though it's precisely because he enunciates it both

ways that we needn't presume that his Jewish joke is an anti-Semitic one.

However for me the most perfect illustration of this same Jewish 'joke' comes to us via the Twitter account of a British comedian, David Baddiel, whose profile identifies him quite simply:

And that seeming banality has the odd effect of functioning like a kind of Rorschach test for the online hoards: at once literal and confounding, it manages somehow to troll the trolls even before they've arrived at the scene. Indeed, Twitter profiles don't get much funnier. Thus, in his stand-up show *My Family: Not the Sitcom* (2016), Baddiel elicits roars of appreciative laughter from his audience when he projects an image of his Twitter by-line onto a large screen. No need, in other words, to follow

convention and name his profession as a 'comedian'
– by naming himself 'Jew' we can already tell he's a
comedian. So it is that Jews, as another British comic,
Sacha Baron Cohen, confirms, 'have a tendency to
become comedians.'

To help us decipher this brainteaser, whereby
the same word is both a joke and not a joke, both a
cordiality and a slur, we might try telling the difference
between the Jewish 'Jew' and the anti-Semitic 'Jew'
this way: whereas an anti-Semite purports to know
exactly what they mean when they say the word *Jew*,
always with the intention of provoking derision or
laughter, Jews couldn't tell you what *Jew* means, they
just know it's funny. And what Jews find particularly
funny about it is linked to the assumption that they
must have some sort of insider's knowledge as to
why it's funny. It's the notion that *they* know what
the difference is that gets them rolling in the aisles.
Because they haven't a clue! Thus knowing that
you *don't* know what Jewish means is what makes
you Jew-ish, just as the repeated discovery of what
you consistently fail to know – especially when it's
something you technically *do*: 'We're all gonna die!'
– is unfailing fodder for the enduring joke. The ha
ha may make us laugh, in other words, but it's the
peculiar that makes us hysterical. Or, as the novelist

Saul Bellow once put it:

> In Jewish stories laughter and trembling are so curi-
> ously intermingled that it is not easy to determine the
> relation of the two.*

Such a curious intermingling is bound to make for
a lot of nervous laughs, lol. But that's not the whole
of it. Failing to tell the difference between laughter
and trembling also makes for something else: the
shuddering sound of a laughter that, at certain points
in life and history, does not quite tell its difference
from a prayer.

PUNCHLINE
Oy vey! *Look* who thinks she knows she knows
nothing.

---

* Saul Bellow's essay 'On Jewish storytelling' appears in Hana Wirth-Nesher
(ed.), *What Is Jewish Literature* (1994).

Index